THE REHABILITATION OF THOMAS MARK

tom crites

headpress

A HEADPRESS BOOK
First published by Headpress in 2020
headoffice@headpress.com

THE REHABILITATION OF THOMAS MARK
The tragic true story of
alcohol, art and loss

Note: Actual names and the names and addresses of
institutions have been changed.

A CIP catalogue record for this book is
available from the British Library

ISBN   978-1-909394-36-0 (paperback)
ISBN   978-1-909394-37-7 (ebook)
No-ISBN hardback

HEADPRESS. POP AND UNPOP CULTURE.

Exclusive NO-ISBN special edition hardbacks and other
items of interest are available at HEADPRESS.COM

Contents

This memoir is dedicated to those
living with depression.

With thanks to Joe and Bonnie,
the greatest friends anyone could
ever have, ever.

'I don't even know why I'm bothering to write this. It isn't like I'm going to ever read it, and I certainly wouldn't see the point of showing it to anybody else. I suppose it's just for the sake of writing, even if it's not very creative or even particularly interesting, at least it's writing.'

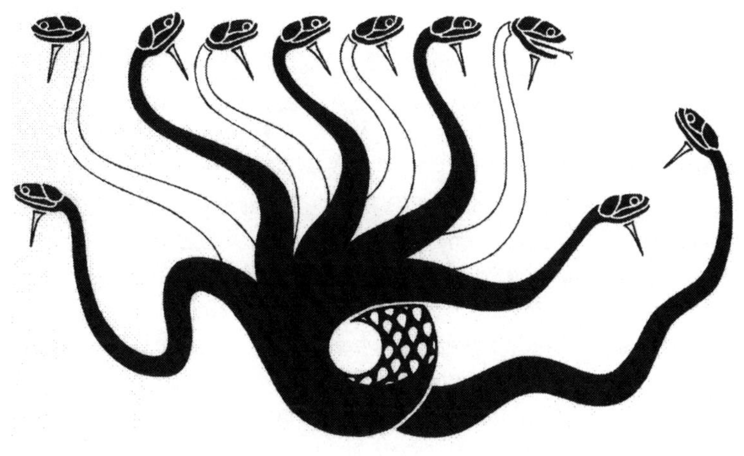

Rehab *First month*

Friday, August 3, 2012

I'd been duped. What I'd been led to believe would be seven to ten days rehab has turned into a months-long rehabilitation. Everybody knew I had it coming, even me. Twenty-five plus years of chronic alcoholism: so many fuck-ups and mistakes, but it only got truly, truly bad over the past three years as unemployment, depression, loneliness and frustration took their toll. A few beers at lunch and drinks around dinner turned into straight alcohol (vodka, whiskey, rum) from the first opening of the eyes on through to blackout. The amount of food eaten declined exponentially in relation to the increased intake of alcohol, and the results were not good: two head injuries resulting from standing pass outs that caused total unconsciousness and required hospital stays, and a face-first fall down a flight of stairs from the top, giving me a scar by my eye that I'll have for a while, blooding my nose, cracking the upper right arm bone, and putting scabs and bruises on all my arms and legs and, along with the constant drunkenness, causing me to miss a trip to Portland to visit the family and see Dad and Linda's great new home.

So, almost the very moment that I agreed to treatment, after more than one person suggested that I might need it (Dad, Joe) I had a tote bag packed for me and a handler/ transporter escort me to the airport (all the way to the gate). There was somebody there waiting to haul me away on an hour-long drive to Treeline Treatment Services, a detox center in the hills (not far from Santa Cruz), and when I did finally reach the facility, I was entering the full throes of withdrawal: seizures, the works. There was a nurse, Rita, who saw to me initially, but it was Abby, the Queen of the Castle, who was to be my primary caregiver over the next few days. I was so shaky and fucked up I could barely even sit up, much less walk; when I did walk, not only did I need a walker, but I needed somebody to help me walk with the walker.

That lasted for days, but with medication (ativan, phenobarbital), hydration (plenty of Gatorade), and three meals a day (each of the three rotating staff members served not only as counselors and caregivers but also as cooks), along with plenty of rest, I gradually improved, which is just shy of miraculous, seeing as how, by all accounts, I was near death. Abby had to check on me multiple times a night at the beginning to ensure that I was still breathing.

Once I was able to get around, after three to four days, I began to appreciate my environment.

Saturday, August 4, 2012

Letters sent today to Joe (re: needs/wants, rants) and Dad (re: status, rent).

Treeline Treatment Services is basically a house. I was a bit surprised when my driver (who took off before I could even think to offer a tip for the timely pick-up and hour-long drive), instead of pulling up at the ER-type entrance of some hospital, pulled into the driveway of a modest-looking single story home with a red painted front door. And the place was actually very nice—much more like a hotel than a traditional detox clinic (at least, as I had imagined). Comfortable, immaculate (thanks to Abby's eye for detail and insistence on cleanliness), and with all of the amenities and more.

For start, they had a large-screen, hi-def, television with a massive cable package, and because for most of my stay I was the sole "client" at Treeline Treatment (aside from one night early on, when Jimmy, from Buffalo, NY, stayed over, but he had what appeared to be some kind of speed-inspired paranoid freak out and accused the entire organization of being a money grubbing Scientology con before picking up and bailing back to Buffalo: and Julius, who arrived a day or two before I left, halfway through an oxycontin detox), I didn't have to share the remote with fucking anybody. There was an exercise machine so fancy I can't even remember the name of it (never used it), and a sweet patio where people could smoke (I've quit) or play cards and watch the ridiculous golfers on the golf course abutting the house chase their balls around.

The staff was entirely female, and they were all amazing. Abby was a great old broad, a wise and caring grandmother, she'd been running (although not in ownership capacity) Treeline Treatment for about three years and had seen over 300 people through detox/withdrawal. And she had a few stories to tell—I kept encouraging her to write a book: having been there myself, I'd really like to read it. It was mentioned by someone, only half in jest, that she might have OCD, as it was not uncommon for her to stay up until the wee hours-rearranging the contents of the cupboards and refrigerator, and, although a kind and compassionate person, she was rather rigorous in her standards when it came to the ladies' cleaning chores. She's the farthest thing from mentally ill however; she just liked things a certain way.

The staff consisted of three women who alternated shifts, splitting each day between two of them (generally), there was Hope, half-Japanese, very cute, very friendly; Libby, a (grand?) mother and baseball fan; and Karen, gorgeous, well-traveled, well read, compassionate... She and I actually became very friendly, despite my inexplicably breaking down in uncontrollable tears in the middle of a conversation the first night I met her, but I rallied and taught her "The Game with no Name" (more on that later). Oh yes, she's a guitar player as well. Oddly, Abby told me once that Karen's only flaw, even though she was the youngest and least experienced member of the staff, was that she didn't interact with the clients enough. Her other job was/is as caregiver for a feisty old lady, but when she was at Treeline Treatment we would literally spend hours playing cards, laughing, joking, making sarcastic and nonsensible remarks, and generally having a really good time just screwing around. Because I was a seizure risk it was suggested/required that I stay for the full initially prescribed ten-day period, so there was plenty of time for the alcohol to leave my system and to start being weaned off the drugs. As a result, I was fairly sharp and clear for about half of my stay, and able to enjoy things like food, company, games, cable TV and walks—Karen took me on some walks around the area that can only be described as magical. In part because I was in her company, the sole person in her company, but also because it's truly amazing how many bizarre, interesting, and beautiful things we found and saw in a single circular route of about a quarter mile:

'The haunted port-a-potty': abandoned on the edge of a field/ crop, this thing is a creepy old orange metal monstrosity, with its Halloween coloration and disturbingly gleaming bone-white commode still in place. Rumor has it that the thing has actually moved over the years. Just out of reach behind a barbed wire fence, it would be great to get over there and photograph any kind of brand logo and put it on hats and t-shirts.

As Karen pointed out, there was a Steinbeck-style scene of a farmer in a tractor plowing his field. From the giant yellow and green beast far out in the field came the strains of country music.

The 'little people palms': among the great variety of flora we saw, the one which amused us the most were these little numbers; Karen pointed them out, and I observed that they might be dwarf palms (man-sized, rather than the traditional sky-scrapers. I think that's a thing, right?). Karen found this amusingly improbable, but in any event we decided that it would be politically incorrect to call them 'dwarf palms', so they became 'little people palms', which for some reason amused us both to no end.

The 'Halloween tree': it's been so long since I read Ray Bradbury's odd, brief book *The Halloween Tree* that I'm not really sure what it was about; a magical and vaguely sinister tree that spirited children away on eerie adventures. At any rate, this tree simply fully embodies the notion of the name the Halloween tree. A huge, ancient, leafless monstrosity with jagged thorny branches twisting out in all directions. Yet it bore what looked like pinecones, though it did not appear to be a pine tree. I could look at that thing every day and not get tired of it.

Even some of the trash we saw was interesting. Plus, I found a dollar bill, just lying on the side of the road. "Lucky Dollah!" (And she makes the best Cobb salad I've ever had. Just had to throw that in.) By the time we got back to the ranch, Karen was so happy and in such a good mood she was singing little people palms songs. I was happy too.

So that was good.

And then there was the game, "The Game with no Name". Taught to me by the limey cat Been Wallers, of the Country Teasers, well over a decade ago, I've taught it to everyone I know. And I have yet to meet anyone who has failed to love it—most people get addicted to it right away. Fast moving, the perfect blend of luck and skill can make you immensely happy or piss you off immeasurably. In short, it's fucking great. Right away I began teaching the ladies how to play. First Karen, then Hope, Libby and finally Abby. They all loved it— Libby even taught her twelve-year-old daughter how to play the game. The great thing about the game is that although there are many fiendish strategies one can employ, at the end it can all come down to luck. So it's not like one person is going to be cleaning clock all day. There can be bad feelings, but these are temporary—everyone wins sometime. And part of the game involves insulting the other players as severely and creatively as possible. When I play with Joe and Bonnie, it is not uncommon for family members and farm animals to be combined. I am my father's legitimate son, but I actually got him to call me a bastard once after a game, I trounced him that badly. It's all about the good feelings. The ladies, however, refused to participate in this aspect of the game; not only were they too ladylike, but they were all technically working while we were playing, despite all the screwing around, they insisted on being professional. So, of course, I couldn't say anything overly rude myself (fucking gentleman call me). Karen and I had one marathon where we literally played all day, except for meals and a (great) walk. That, I believe, was on a Thursday or Friday—and I looked forward, with no small amount of eager anticipation, to seeing her again all weekend long (her next shift being Monday). Julius arrived Sunday night however, so I didn't have Karen all to myself when she came around Monday, and we didn't get our special walk (need for supervision, medication, regular meal times), but we still got to play multiple rounds and have a grand time. She seemed pleased when I told her I'd been looking forward to that all weekend.

To Dad fm Tom

Hello! Just wanted to let you know I'm doing fine—much better in fact. The people here are terrific, incredibly kind and helpful. They stopped the seizures almost immediately, and completely prevented the usual vomiting associated with withdrawal. I've been getting hydrated and gaining weight and am in better health than in months past.

I will be at the address on the envelope until next Tuesday, after which time I will be transferred to another facility, Oakview Recovery, for which I do not have the address. I'm not sure if they'll even allow mail. I'm told the extensive rehabilitation they offer may take three to six months—I had no idea. At any rate, I've asked Joe to forward you my mail, if you could take care of the bills while I'm gone I'd appreciate it. Keep a tab and let me know the balance. (Thank you, by the way, for taking care of the bills I left unpaid on the kitchen table—Armand mentioned it to me. He's a pretty good guy.)

I'm sure this is all costing you a fortune—I don't know if I'll ever be able to pay you back, but I will try. (Thanks, by the way, for arranging for the transporter—that cat took me all the way to the gate.)

I think that just about covers it. I can't thank you enough, for everything.

Love,
Tom

P.S.—you might want to let Lisa C know that I'm getting treatment—I know she was concerned.

To Dad fm Tom

Dear Dad,

Just wanted to make sure things are lined up for the coming months. I was led to believe the rehab process would only take seven to ten days, but the actual rehabilitation will take three to six months. Had I known that, once I agreed to treatment I still would have come, but I would have made arrangements. Like clearing out the refrigerator, doing laundry, chipping some of the frost and ice away from the icebox in the fridge... would have packed a few more items of clothing as well. Also, I'm not sure how I took two shuttles and a plane with only $39.00 in my pocket. Hopefully the trip back, which, apparently, may be up to half a year away, will be as smooth as the trip here. With a little more advance notice, I would have taken more prompt action toward replacing my missing ATM card; without phone or internet access, I won't be able to check on my account.

At any rate, I understand you've already been in contact with Armand, and I'm sure he's relayed this information. But just to reiterate:

Rent of $825.00 is due on the first of each month, payable to: Smile Properties 1, and submitted to:

Ocean Realty Management
640 W. 8th St.
Long Beach, CA
90804

Please keep tab of rent and bills that accrue (not sure if I'm using that word correctly) and I will do what I can upon my return. At the moment I am still at Treeline Treatment, but early next week I will be transferring to the following location:

Oakview Recovery
432 Treeline Rd
Santa Cruz, CA
95060

The stay here has been truly rejuvenating; I've gained twelve pounds in about a week. I am well on my way to becoming a great fat bastard. As I remain the sole "client" at Treeline Treatment at this time, and all of the counselors are women, I am being spoiled rotten. I do not want to leave.

Armand has shown me some photos of Oakview, and it looks like a beautiful area. Although the prospect of confronting all of my issues and history in a state of full consciousness, without the safety blanket of alcohol, does inspire a touch of anxiety. But, here's hoping it's all for the best.

I think that about covers it; love to Rhys and Linda, and

Love,
Tom

THE REHABILITATION OF THOMAS MARK

To Margaret fm Tom

Dear Margaret,

Hello! Hope all well out your way—as Dad may have mentioned, I'll be doing a stint in rehab. I've just been through the detox process for chronic alcoholism, and will be transferring to long-term rehabilitation soon. It's supposed to be a fairly nice facility (I hope so, as it appears I will be there for months), but the notion of confronting my issues and history without the security blanket of alcohol does inspire some apprehension. So, as my PC crashed months ago, and for some reason Dell's customer service contractors refused to send me a catalog, and I won't have phone or internet access for months to come, it will/may seem like I've fallen off the edge of the world: I haven't, but I've come close to it. This was a long time coming, but hopefully it will do some good. The next head injury could be the last one...

At any rate, the people here are great, they really helped me out during the first days of withdrawal and seizures and have been just indescribably helpful and kind. Not only am I the only "client" at this clinic at the moment, which is so nice it's like having my own private hotel, but all of the counselors are women so I've been getting spoiled rotten. So, so far rehab is a good thing. Hope the next stage is just as positive.

Once again, hope all well out your way... Oh yeah, for the foreseeable future my address will be:

> *Oakview Recovery*
> *432 Treeline Rd*
> *Santa Cruz, CA*
> *95060*

> *Cheers to Bruce, and,*
> *Love*
> *Tom*

tom crites

To Tom fm Margaret

HELLO TOM!!

Yes, Dad did tell me that you're doing rehab. In fact, just this afternoon, he passed your address along to me, so your letter had perfect timing.

I read about the facility online. I like that it's not a religious or twelve-step based program. I find with those programs, it is too easy for people to swap out one addiction for another without really figuring anything out. I think it's funny that you're the only client at the moment. I don't know when you've ever been the center of attention, and I bet you're just charming all those women.

I know facing the past, figuring out shit, and making a plan for the future can be really overwhelming. But, you're too decent and talented a person to waste yourself on booze/head injuries. If there is anything I can do to help, please don't hesitate to ask. Really. Dad gave me the name of the patient advocate person. If you wanted me to call her and fill in some of the childhood crap, I will do it. Or, if you want to keep up correspondence, I'll be happy to do that too. Or, whatever else you think of that might help.

Bruce and I are well. The school year starts soon, and Bruce is dreading it. He really hates his job. And, the administrators seem to be more self-interested than committed to the school. We're planning on another trip to New Orleans for fall break and probably Christmas too. It is the place where I can relax.

Please write back. I love you. MC

To Dad fm Tom

Hello—here's hoping this letter finds you and the family well, and the new house is breaking in and decorating well also. Again, I am sorry that I did not make the planned visit, but there will be ample opportunity in the future.

I left Treeline Treatment with some sadness on Tuesday the 31ˢᵗ, and after a few days quarantined in the "withdrawal cabin", which is apparently standard operating procedure, I have moved down onto "campus" and begin my course work tomorrow. My estimated date of completion is mid-November, but of course this is not set in stone. It will be somewhat more challenging than I expected (although I really did not know quite what to expect), and take somewhat longer as well.

But I am encouraged by the fact that much of the staff, who for the most part, seem competent and knowledgeable, were "students" here themselves and not only got enough out of the program to turn their lives around, but enjoyed it so much they decided to stay and help others do the same. I've read multiple "success stories" from other students from multiple phases of the program, which also provide encouragement. So I am hopeful.

If you would, can you please contact Joe and see/confirm if he can make the trip to the apartment on a weekly basis and not only check the mail for notifications from Ocean Realty, but be on the lookout for notices posted on the door. If you could also contact Lisa C and ask that she keep an eye on this as well I would be much obliged. And, although I have given them both your cell number (in case of home emergency) please confirm that they have this.

*Joe Salvers: (626) 223-**xxxx***
*Lisa Conrad: (310) 672-**xxxx***

*I do not wish to put anyone to inconvenience, but for now I am unable to handle certain things directly. Lisa will also be able to confirm Ocean Realty's address and phone number, so please ask her to do so. The phone number I have with me for Ocean is (562) 436-**xxxx**, although this is the number related to their old address, I believe they kept this the same, but again Lisa can confirm. If she is out of town or otherwise unavailable, try Johnny at (562) 234-**xxxx**. My worst nightmare is coming back to find the apartment cleaned out, and I have seen Ocean post "three day notice to pay or quit" tags on* *people's doors, so please follow up and keep abreast of this.*

In reviewing some of the Oakview materials, it appears that Oakview is a wing of Narconon, a program developed by a gentleman in Arizona State Prison, based on the theories of one L. Ron Hubbard. Interesting. However, I am assured that no attempts at indoctrination will be made.

(Narconon and the Narconon logo are trademarks and service marks owned by the association for Better Living and Education International.)

Thank you very much for sending the check to fund my "student" account. I've asked Joe to also send me my checkbook, as we have to purchase just about everything except toilet paper and paper towels (and food), although they do provide unlimited envelopes and stamps, which is rather thoughtful of them. And I've asked him to send some more clothing and other items—half a tote bag will not be sufficient for a stay of around four months, I'm afraid.

I think that's it for now. I will have no Internet access for the coming months, as I believe I may have mentioned before, although after a "ten-day blackout restriction" there will be limited phone access. But this will be somewhat tricky... at any rate, love to Linda and Rhys, and,

Love
Tom

Sunday, August 5, 2012

The ten-day observation and medication period ended Tuesday, July 31. My withdrawal symptoms were completely gone, I'd put on about twelve pounds in a week thanks to regular meals and good nutrition. I had been weaned off the phenobarbital, was in as good a shape mentally and physical as I had been in a long time, and I met some really sweet ladies who, I believe, I can consider friends. Got a very nice card from Abby, a great hug and good words of encouragement from Karen, and Libby in particular said she wanted to know when I'd be coming for a visit, a threat I promised and plan to make good on. I did not want to leave. Hugs and good words from Abby as well. And I was out of Treeline Treatment, being driven to what would be my home of improvement for the perhaps the rest of the year.

But first, the withdrawal cabin. On a hill above the main campus, this is literally a cabin; three rooms of bunk beds, kitchen, main room, M & F bathrooms... and that's it. All 'students' coming to Oakview first get essentially quarantined in the cabin until their piss tests are clean and any withdrawal symptoms have disappeared. No television, no games, no caffeine, no sugar, no going outside alone, no washcloths. What they do have are TRs (Training Routines), "light objectives", exercises, and walks; lots of walks, sometimes three times a day. Food (meals) was brought to us three times a day, and there was always fresh fruit, yogurt, jello, breads, chips, etc. And the meals are actually pretty fine. My first night we had Alaskan king crab legs, grilled chicken, fried peppers and onions and more. A daily regimen of vitamins in horse pill and beverage form.

Also available are the "nerve assist" and "the body calm", half assed techniques that are somewhat like, but not quite, massage. Actually I shouldn't say half assed; a number of people came through the cabin while I was there, people who hadn't the luxury of detoxing/withdrawal in a comfortable environment prior to arriving at Oakview, and as Oakview is a wing of Narconon there was no medication, only physical therapy, and it seemed to do many of them some amount of good. But they bugged the shit out of me, the "body calm" especially. You lie there and the counselor/therapist basically works their way down your body, pressing and releasing (Feel my hands? Good.). Way too clinical and methodical for me. The "nerve assist" isn't much better, as the C/T runs their hands down various parts of your body with moves that are like massage, but again, not quite massage. And they refuse to vary the routine—I was a little sore in certain areas (calf, feet, back) from all the hiking (it's not a truly mountainous area, but it's definitely got a little altitude and some varied/hilly terrain) and the guy said he couldn't alter his pattern to focus on them at all. (And that was a day of three walks and four objectives!) I tried two nerve assists and one body calm, and called them both off.

It is an interesting area—there's a forest of massive eucalyptus trees just up the hill a bit that looks truly bitchin' and primeval when the tops are shrouded in fog. Lots of fauna as well: saw several deer, multiple species of birds, a skunk, a fox... local legend has it that there's a big mountain lion wandering around as well, and numerous people claim to have seen bobcats (fuck, this page is a mess—I'm falling asleep but I can't take a nap because it's almost dinner time and I got shit for sleep last night so want to be sure and save it for tonight.)

Withdrawal Cabin:

    no washcloths
littered bedroom floors; earplug, hairpin, Kleenex
bags not checked and delivered for days
no protective toilet seat covers, in either bathroom
staff cell phones going off during nerve assists
terrible lighting in men's bathroom
(forced) hikes/walks for students w/o proper attire (shoes/
boots, hats)
awkward/unhelpful physical therapy

The light objectives pissed me off at first, but after a few different rounds with a few different counselors, I began to get the point: the here and the now, "being there," in the moment, in the world: there are many, many other things in your environment besides just yourself. At least, I think that's the point.

At any rate, on Friday, August 3rd, I had my final interview regarding my willingness and ability to come down and start the program. My urine was clean enough (traces of residual TNC, which they don't worry about too much because that stays in your system for weeks or months (a benzocoiaze...?) which was probably the phenobarbital I'd been getting at Treeline Treatment for the seizures. I'd done something like eleven light objectives (I'd been told it generally took "about eight" but was different for everyone), eating and sleeping well, and my attitude was good. At least my anonymous "case supervisor" thought so, and that afternoon I was "coming down the mountain!" And dropped right into a lengthy very personal history interview. Not a problem really, as I'd been having those since I first consented to treatment. But like bills, they never seem to end. The rest of the afternoon/evening was getting oriented, learning the routines and how to find my way around, dinner, and settling in.

On Saturday I began learning the routine. After breakfast there's roll call and chore assignment. I pulled "kitchen" (actually just the serving area), dining area, a main entryway with a crew of four or five (it went pretty quickly, and all I had to do was sweep while someone else mopped up behind me).

Then a barrage of tests. First, an IQ test, then an aptitude test, then the Oxford Capacity test, and a "tone scale questionnaire." Fun, fun, fun, break for lunch. Met with ethics. There was a brief "therapeutic training routines" course introduction, then into the course and begin training, Learning Book 1 (of 8). Which at this point, meaning as far as I made it today, is pretty much the same as what was being done at the cabin. And by then it was 7:30 PM and time for "muster" (group meeting/pep talk of the "wins"). Then, upon the strong suggestion of my supervisor, Danny, I began working through the "sauna book".

"Clear body, clear mind" by Mr. L. Ron Hubbard, founder of Scientology, and while Narconon does not hide its origins, it does not appear to push any Scientology agenda. I was wondering where Jimmy got that idea... And soon, after working through a few "demonstrations" on the value of sauna as a way to rid the body of accumulated toxins/poisons (drugs, pollution, etc.), it was 9:45 PM and I only got halfway through. But, it needs to be done before Book 1 is complete in order to begin the sauna program. Which people really do rave about, and according to Mr. Hubbard, the release of those toxins can re-engage or trigger their effects upon the mind, so I may have flashbacks to look forward to. That's quite enough for one day, thank you. Did I mention that I currently have a room to myself? Nice way to ease in—no previously established "house rules". There's a color television with digital receiver and antenna that I can't get to work, but the clock radio gets what is it?—KCSB I think, a station with a wildly varied programming schedule. So that's all right. Not total silence—there was <u>nothing</u> at the cabin. I wrote a P.S. on the envelope I sent to Joe asking for more stuff, asking for an iPod, loaded, that I can get Sam and Armand to add to. Here's hoping...

Okay, we're up to date. It's Sunday and I'm writing about Sunday. But wait, forgot about the Target run of yesterday; every week one can submit a "store order form" for up to $150 of goods from Target that will be purchased and delivered, assuming one has funds in their student account, that is. The old man, who is paying for rehab (which, according to Admissions paper work, is the equivalent of an annual middle-class salary—$35.5K!), was kind enough to send in $100 so I could purchase some essentials, which I truly needed. Oakview supplies TP, paper towels and garbage bags, and you can have all the envelopes and stamps you want, but everything else has to be purchased by the students: soap, shampoo, toothpaste, towels, washcloths, even coat hangers. There are still many things I need, but I got the basic toiletries, notebook, wristwatch, etc. Already got the next one working, just have to hope my checkbook comes via priority mail in time to fund this. Moving on. Sunday, Sunday. Roll call is pushed back to 10:00 AM, but instead of a ten to fifteen minutes chore, this is the day that the student body conducts white glove cleaning of the entire campus. So, spent nearly an hour wiping down the microwave, drink dispensers, ice machine, and service table. Was through, received compliments. Then it's on to room cleaning, according to a strict checklist. The room had been kept in fair shape, but had not been entirely clean when I moved in: there was trash in both waste baskets, junk in the drawers (including a tape dispenser belonging to reception, since returned to Ned), stains and splatters on walls and doors, and w/o a roommate, I was cleaning until nearly 3:00 PM—all right 2:30, with a break for lunch. Most of the rest of the day spent reading and writing, and being interrupted nearly a dozen times by counselors knocking on the door and poking their heads in to "check" on me (as they apparently do with everyone). One lady even came by when I was nekkid in the bathroom, getting ready to pull one off and grab a shower (have to stagger the showers). Still waiting on more clothes from home, which will be a little while coming, and currently have only three sets of socks and underwear and one towel (on loan from the sauna). And each room only gets one laundry day a week, mine is Friday. Fairly tired after three hours sleep and more hours than that of cleaning. Lights out by 10:00 PM.

To Tom fm Dad

Hello Thomas,

So good to hear from you. Glad they are treating you well, and that your health is responding. It's not a twelve-step program and hopefully the results will be better. Take all the time there you need, it doesn't cost any more for six months than six weeks.

I talked to Lisa and Johnnie before I left Long Beach, so they know you'll be gone for a while. They were very supportive and delighted to hear that you are getting some assistance. I'll write them (the phone number I have doesn't work) with an update.

I took care of a few things before leaving town. Emptied the perishables out of the fridge (though I didn't try to do anything about the iceberg, that fridge is a piece of shit). Took out some garbage, made sure everything was turned off and did as much laundry as I had quarters for. Joe went by a few days later and tossed out some more stuff he didn't think would last and is sending me a package with more clothes and your laptop (scheduled to arrive here Thursday). He said he would check your mail periodically and send it to me. I'll take care of the bills, toss the porn, and send on any personal stuff to you.

The cost is nothing; between my first-born and a BMW, the automakers can go out of business. Your health and future are more important to me than anything I could buy.

Love
Dad

Monday, August 6, 2012

Awaken 5:15 AM by a knock on the door. It was Charles, the night man—he'd seen a car on the security cameras and was wondering if anybody had been in my room. Of course there wasn't. He apologized and left, but now I was awake. Got up, took a shit, wrote a bit, grabbed some yogurt, tea and an apple, went back to my room until 7:00 AM when the "lights out" period ended. No water left in the dispenser, so tried a cup of coffee, first one in a long time. Didn't crank me out like it used to, I think I just made it too strong when I made it at home. Hung around until breakfast: breakfast burritos, potato wedges, sausage, bacon, and fruit. Now just waiting for roll call and chores, and then it's onto the course work. Today I think we'll get into "bull baiting". And we did get to that and a number of other "therapeutic training routine course" exercises as well; "confronting", "delivering a communication", "acknowledgements", "half-acknowledgements", "the cycle of communication" and "originations".

This went on until 7:30 PM, with breaks for lunch and dinner, and a brief snack and mail call break (got a very nice letter from sister Margaret, with a card stating "please take care of yourself" and a picture of a monkey on it). "Muster" (assembly) at 8:00 PM, and as I'm taking the night course in preparation for the sauna program, I was doing that from 8:15-9:45. And I still didn't finish it, despite spending that same period of time Saturday night. Looks like I'll be back tomorrow... When that ended I was too tired to think straight, but went back to my room and managed to write a letter to Margaret before passing out at 11:15.

To Margaret fm Tom

Dear Margaret,

Hello, and thank you so much for your letter! It's always good to hear from you, but especially in here. I have transferred from Treeline Treatment, the detox facility (I really didn't want to go—that was the life! Got along so well with those wonderful ladies). After a brief mandatory quarantine in the "withdrawal cabin" (S.O.P.) have come down the mountain to the main campus and begun coursework. Right now it's therapeutic "TRs") teaching the "3 Cs" (confront, control, and communicate); I'm "twinned" (partnered up) with an adorable little tattooed punk rock girl, and we're making progress and having some laughs at the same time. And I'm not sure what I expected, but for some reason I thought it would be, well, easier (don't ask me why...). After breakfast there's a 9:00 AM roll call and chore assignment. Course work begins at 10:00 AM, and continues until 7:30 PM (with meal breaks and some free time around them, plus one snack and mail call break). I'm also doing the night courses, which run until 9:45 PM. All of which makes for a pretty long damn day.

But the facility is nice enough, the grounds are pretty (lots of fruit trees) and the place is located between the... well it's hard to tell, we're not allowed to roam too far, but it's not quite the mountains and definitely not the valleys; ten miles from the ocean... let's call it the "high hills". Lots of wild life: while up at the cabin we had to take a lot of walks, and on top of loads of deer and wild, but friendly, cats, we saw skunk and fox, neither of which I'd seen in the wild before. The other students here seem generally friendly; not only is it universally recognized among the student body that we're all in the same boat for pretty much the same reason, but there are definite penalties for a range of clearly defined levels of offenses against the facility's code of conduct.

I am finding encouragement in the fact that in speaking with many different counselors and staff members here, the majority of them have told me that they themselves went through this rehabilitation program, and not only did it help them turn their lives around, but they liked it so much they decided to stay and help others do the same. Encouraging.

About the facility and its program... come to find out, Oakview is one wing of Narconon (from "Narcotics none"), an institutional program based on the work of one L. Ron Hubbard, developed by a gentleman from the Arizona State Prison system... But, I have made sure to make multiple inquires and have been assured multiple times that no attempts at indoctrination will be made. And although L.Ron's name keeps popping up, I haven't yet seen a single Scientology text. Still weird though...

Oh yeah, the food's pretty decent, too.

Um... I think that's about it. Hope this wasn't too scattered, it's been a very long day that started at 5:15 AM when the night desk watch woke me up to ask if I'd had any visitors in my room because he saw a car on one of the surveillance cameras... wha?

Tom

P.S.—Feel free to drop me a line any time! Like I say, it's not all bad and I'm embracing the process and the positive change I hope it will bring about, but the place has very definite rules. Let's just say I won't be getting out much for a while... It is kind of an institution, after all.

To Tom fm Margaret

Dear Tom:

Thanks for the letter. I was hoping we could keep this writing thing up.

Hmmm, L. Ron based stuff. Yeah, I'd be concerned about the cult aspects. However, I have also read (can't say how truthful or propagandistic it was) that one thing the scientologist do fairly well is dealing with substance abuse. And, aside from his ego and bizarre followers, L. Ron was an interesting and creative mind. Having done the five-minute research quest on the interwebs, I do see there is criticism of the parties behind the scenes. However, there aren't that many non-twelve-step programs out there, people tend to have a vast array of abilities to think, reason, and express themselves (and I'm pretty biased against twelve-step programs because of their emphasis on being powerless), and I think different approaches make sense to different people. I do like that there seems to be an emphasis on making your body healthy as well as learning personal control/communication. I think that ultimately you have to decide if you embrace the foundation ideas of the program as well as make sense of it for yourself in a way that ultimately leads to you being healthy and living more of what you want.

I'd be concerned if they started telling you to abandon your family, your talents, and the core of who you are.

I appreciate getting a snapshot of your day. It does sound long, and if you're in close quarters with a bunch of folks who are also in the same boat, I can see that you can either bond or butt heads. I used to say in college, you put rats in a cage, eventually they are going to bite each other. However, swift and consistent response helps maintain order. And, isn't all of life kinda a big game of rules?

I suspect your taste and mine are fairly different when it comes to books and movies and music, so give me some guidance on your tastes. Have you read The Girl with the Dragon Tattoo series yet? They are fairly violent and sexual, but I enjoyed the series. What is considered forbidden where you are? Caffeine? Sugar? Tobacco? Where do your candy leanings head? Sour? Fruit? Chocolate? Strange oriental delights?

You asked about the grandparents. I don't know what Dad has told you. It's bad, but not as bad as it might have been. Granny has reached the stage where she cannot be left alone or handled by one person. Cathy has been named her guardian. Currently Cathy would like to start with arranging for in-home assistance for Granddaddy. If that doesn't work, I think the next step is to force them into a nursing facility. Granddaddy has said that he will go to a nursing facility if Granny goes. She is tremendously dependent upon Granddaddy and I wouldn't want to work in a facility that was housing her but not him.

I'm trying really hard to let go of being frustrated with Granddaddy. Everyone tried to convince him years ago that allowing people to help wouldn't be the end of the world... And his stubbornness has led to what does amount to the end of the world in their eyes. That might be a good lesson for all of us to embrace now, that asking for/ accepting help isn't the worst thing you can do. Sometimes, refusing the help is the worst thing.

I'm looking forward to hearing from you again. So, what about this punk rocker girl?

Love,
Margaret

Tuesday, August 7, 2012

Not a particularly splendid day. Not horrible, but not great. Tired for large part of the day, even with seven hours sleep: ate fruit and salad, took vitamins (ate a lot of greasy shit too) but was spilling shit all day, had bad hair (didn't bother me when I was drunk and could wear a hat everywhere—no hats in class here), was generally uninspired. And got no mail, and was completely demoralized when I learned that we would have to repeat that first set of seven hours over and over again for <u>days</u>. Like I said, demoralized. And my neighbor, right next door told me his room has bedbugs. Great—if that's true, <u>my</u> room will soon have bedbugs. And, I was in night class tonight again until 9:45 PM. <u>AND</u> not only do I still have the "final essay" on the "clean and clear body" deal to finish, but I realized/was informed that there will be additional reading, and another essay, and another "demo to supervisor" on the wonders of "twinning" (partnering up). Fuck me. So tired. Not happy. And as always, still alone in the crowd. But the day was not entirely without its small accomplishments and successes:

Mailed a letter to Margaret

Submitted a "student request form" to initiate a subscription to the *Los Angeles Times*

Submitted a "maintenance request form" to have my room "bombed" to try and nip the bedbug issue in the bud

Got a sketchbook from Mr. Armand (can't recall whether I've already mentioned him or not: He works in the front office (admissions?) and is liaison between Oakview and Treeline Treatment—he helped me out when I was there, sending out mail, picking up items I needed, etc. Taught him the game with no name as well—loves it

The big guy, Tom, who came to the withdrawal cabin shortly before I left, and who snores like a drunken polar bear, came down from the cabin but didn't (immediately at least) get put in my room. When I returned a book Armand had loaned me (*Clown Girl* by Monica Drake, which was quite good: the lady has a way with word play) and Abby's beard trimmers, I added a note of thanks and stuff, including the suggestion that Tom might be a better match for another snorer in the thirty-five-plus housing unit (AKA the ghetto, the old folks home) than myself

More to say, but it's past 10:30 now, and supposed to have lights out by 11:00 PM and I'd like to get some reading in.
Tired, depressed, questioning the entire situation.

To Margaret fm Tom

Dear Margaret,

CHEERS! Many thanks for your letter—as I may have mentioned before, I've always appreciated and enjoyed letters more than emails: more personal and sincere, plus it's just fun to get mail! Especially here! (You'll have to forgive me if I repeat myself—not having my letters stored on a PC, I don't always remember what I said last time...)
Yeah, the L. Ron Hubbard thing was a bit of a surprise, but aside from the little blurbs on the course materials (based on the book <u>Clear Body, Clear Mind—Sauna Program</u>; "Based on the theories of...") ol' L. Ron is really never brought up. And so far Scientology hasn't even really been mentioned, except for during the entry interviews where they wanted to make it clear what the origins of Narconon were (and those weren't specifically Scientology, apparently the founder of this

program just found L. Ron inspiring), got to give them credit for not trying to hide it and spring it out on the unsuspecting "students" (we're not "patients" or "clients" here, we're "students"—although during the more frustrating moments I think of us as inmates interred at the therapy gulag...) midway or late during the course.

Dad was unaware of the L. Ron connection as well. But, people literally come from all over the country to attend one of the Narconon Centers (there's one in Tahoe and another in Placerville). The L. Ron connection did bother one cat who stayed briefly at Treeline Treatment—he came all the way from Buffalo, NY, to go through detox at Treeline Treatment and rehab at Oakview; he stayed one night at T.T., then freaked out over the L. Ron/Scientology angle and the "money grubbing" associated with it all. So far, not an issue, really, as far as I can tell.

Been named IC ("in charge") of morning dining/serving area cleaning crew! My IQ test indicates that I have lost a few points since childhood (age, substance abuse, head injuries...) but am still "above average"; got my sauna certificate and working toward finishing the first course book so I can start the sauna/exercise/supplement program, which is touted as a regimen that can break up and remove toxin/drug/chemical deposits that build up in the body—side effects: hives, reactivation of previous conditions, and flashbacks!

You don't need to feel obliged to send anything out—I'm just kind of frustrated over the fact that I embarked upon what looks to be a four-month journey with only half a bag of clothes, one pair of shoes, one hat, and no books. (Have borrowed and read a couple ones though: Clown Girl by Monica Drake, a lady who really has a way with wordplay, and a couple by Dean Koontz, a sorta horror author who I'd never read before.) Did read the first two Dragon Tattoo books, and saw the movies: don't know why they're such a big deal. Some interesting characters and scenes, but just so... damn... LONG... But I do generally prefer weird or classical fiction when I read. Re-read Ed Abbey's The Monkey Wrench Gang lately, and as far as non-fiction, God's Middle Finger by Richard Grant is excellent. Highly recommended! The only things absolutely prohibited here, *aside from drugs, alcohol, and weapons of course, is pornography in any form. But as far as the written word, the more bizarre the better. They have coffee, tea and sugar (and occasionally ice cream) here, but you can't have cash or credit cards in your possession, so there aren't any vending machines or anything like that; you have to have money in your "student account" and fill out a "store order form" for the weekly Target run. Which is always a toss-up apparently, because you can't get online to check and see what they have in stock. (You can get online for special needs/requests, but you have to fill out a "student request form", get <u>four</u> signatures approving the request, then try to catch one of the Ethics Officers, make an appointment, and have them get online to look into what you need –rrrr...)*

My sweet tooth, which I did not have previously, comes back with a vengeance whenever I quit smoking (which I have done). I find I like just about everything, and each time I hoof it up and through Cambodia town in L.B. I always get a couple bags (or more) of strange Asian candy, some of which have absolutely no English on the manufacture's packaging.

At the moment I'm not seeing much practical benefit in the program, aside from keeping me "off the streets" for the time being— there are alternating moments of beauty and depression, but I'm hoping that once I get going in the sauna program I'll feel a little more clear and intent. Haven't had to freak out yet, as I understand some people do...

Not a whole lot to say about the young lady—she's nice enough and all, friendly enough, messed up sense of humor like myself, substance abuser like myself, twenty-two years younger than myself. I did get pretty lucky on the twin draw in that regard however, as one of the "training routines" is supposed to teach one how to just "be there comfortably" when confronting another person involves just sitting across from each other about three feet apart and simply looking the other person in the eyes for an extended period of time in utter motionless silence (my record: twenty-five minutes). And instead of staring at some broken down old drunk like myself, I get to gaze at the face of a beautiful young girl. So, I guess I can't, or shouldn't, rather, complain too much. Whether the program "sticks" or not, I'll still feel somewhat guilty over the fact that Dad chose to pay a ridiculous amount of money for the entire detox/rehab program.

Anyway, enough for now, hope all continues to flow smoothly in your part of the world, cheers to all, and,

Love,
Tom

To Dad fm Tom

Dear Dad,

Hello! Good to hear from you—hope all continues to go well with the new digs, and you are finding P-land agreeable. Still getting used to things here in the land of Narconon: full schedules (seven hours of courses most days, plus another one-and-three-quarters if you're taking the night classes, which I have been), daily chores plus weekly "white glove" cleaning of rooms and the entire "campus," a multi-page "Codes of Conduct" package listing multiple levels of offenses and the associated penalties, rules, restrictions, curfew, "lights out" time... quite the change from sitting in front of the television all day with a drink in hand. But, that's no good, so at the moment I'll embrace the alternative. People generally friendly and helpful, and the area is pretty nice, so, could be worse places to spend a chunk of the year.

W/O all this saved on a word processing program I can't be quite sure what information/news I've already relayed, so you'll have to excuse any redundancy. Speaking of PCs, I'm not sure why Joe is sending you the laptop—?—I don't even think those are allowed here for the students, as they might contain "restricted" material, and in any case there is no internet or printer access for we "students". So, if this reaches you before you receive the laptop and/or before you forward the package of clothes and whatever else Joe is sending to you (another thing I'm not clear on—why is he sending my clothes to you? I've sent him this address—haven't heard from him yet, though...). There really is no need to send the laptop down to me here. Many thanks for coordinating with him; I hate being so far out of the loop and having to constantly ask yet more and more favors from people who have already done so much for me, but hopefully this time it will pay off. Thanks as well for taking care of the "little things around the house." The days before detox were, I admit, a bit blurry and non-productive. And yet, that refrigerator should have been replaced decades ago. That freezer compartment has never worked properly—last time I remember seeing one frost over that badly was at Cedar Drive in Livermore.

Got a very nice supportive letter from Margaret, and have been sending letters as often as possible to try and stay somewhat in touch with the outside world. The TV doesn't work and they don't get the paper here (I did submit a request to subscribe to the <u>Los Angeles Times</u>, but haven't received the A-OK on that yet), but I have sent Joe my apartment mailbox key and my PO Box key, as well as giving people the address here, so hope to be able to maintain a semblance of communication.

If anything truly alarming arises, I believe you've been in contact with Armand and Lisa here at Oakview, and you can get word to me through them.

Feel like there was something else I wanted to say, but it's late night, long day, so I'll sign off. My thanks to you for everything, and I will keep you posted.

Love,
Tom

P.S.—If any of the mail that Joe forwards consists of balance transfer checks related to my credit cards (probably only Wells Fargo, but Citi may send some as well), please forward those to me here. I will use them to fund my student account, and try and compensate Joe for mileage and postage. Thank you!

Wednesday, August 8, 2012

Almost seven hours sleep. Woke up in not the best of spirits. Did the morning thing, yogurt (w/granola), shower, breakfast, and trudged off for the chores and eight-and-a-quarter hours of coursework, which actually went fairly well: Jackie and I made it through all eight of the first training routines in Book 1 two-and-a-half times. The "bull bait" TR actually encourages you to insult your twin in order to find and push their buttons and get a reaction. Along the way many of our ridiculous comments, and of those around us, were profanity-laden perversions of imagined personal histories—often the entire room (only about eight to ten people today) would break up over something one of the twinships said. We even had to have the supervisor, Danny, make a ruling on one comment involving a fire poker being stuck up someone's (mine) ass. So, it's not all complete drudgery.

Finished the "clear body, clear mind" program, even though it took me four nights to complete what most people apparently accomplish in an hour... Guess I just like writing too much... at any rate, it's finished now.

No mail today; been here at Oakview for almost ten days, after ten days at Treeline Treatment, and the only letter I got was from my sister, Margaret. Send me some mail, fuckers!

New roommate today—we'll see how that goes. We could be shacked up together for months. Gotta beat the younger kids' quarters up around the main office—noisy area with up to four "students" per room. <u>That</u> would suck some ass. Like I said, we'll see. Oh yeah—it is that cat Tom, and it turns out we both snore.

Roomate:

Started complaining first night
Loud guitar playing/singing
Urinating w/bathroom door & front window open

tom crites

Clips toenails directly onto floor, leaves them there
Leaves tracks/spills of foot powder all over floor; feet stink
Slamming doors before 6:30 AM
Leaves windows by bed open all night (weight problem
causes overheating)
Walked off daily chore duty after refusing to handle tasks
Half-ass white glove room clean
Inability to comprehend simple tasks (as with clothes day);
instead of turning radio off, switched it to alarm buzzer—
went off at midnight
Helps self to items not owned
Constant complaining
Won't clean own shit from toilet
Tunes TV up loud enough to hear outside
Farts regularly in room, even when asleep
Cursing inanimate objects at 5:30 AM

To Tom fm Dad

Hi Tom,

Joe sent some of your clothes, and here they are.

I wrote Ocean and told them you were in the hospital for a while and that I would be sending the rent check, so they should be happy. I've asked Joe to watch out for any notices just in case (can't get through on Lisa's phone number).

Things have gotten much worse with my parents. Court orders, fleeing from justice, etc. Mrs. Rahm handled the end of life so well, it's distressing to see my parents handling it so poorly.

Couple books—a different take on the Joseph bible story and M. Atwood, a beautiful writer.

Love,
Dad

Thursday, August 9, 2012

Awake a little before 6:00 AM. Pissed, back to bed, lay there for a while, got up around 6:00 AM and went up to the main building for tea and granola. And to get some earplugs for me and the roommate. Condensed my music request list for when/if I get an iPod or other listening device. Started a letter to Joe, hope to make it one wherein I don't ask for any favors. Had a brief talk with Tom re: the snoring ("You are not my friend!" being one of the first things he said to me this morning), but as we're both fairly reasonable cats it should be workable. And I am being proactive, what with the earplugs—the night man, Charles, said that nose strips are also available but he didn't have any immediately on hand. Had breakfast (breakfast burritos, bacon, sausage, tator tots, fruit, OJ, tea).

Back to the room before roll call and chores. On the way was brought up short; there was just a bit of fog lingering (this around 8:15 AM) and from behind the eucalyptus forest the sun was shining through, between the leaves and branches, creating an array of sunbeams. A true moment of beauty. And one that almost made up for a development just moments before that was less that sterling—my positive work ethic may have fucked me here: as I was leaving the main building after breakfast the student IC (student in charge) asked for a moment, and said there was a daily chore that wasn't getting done well and would I mind taking that on instead of sweeping, as he knew I'd do a good job. "Sure I said, what is it?" "Course (room) bathroom." D'oh! In yet another example of life's glorious ironies, I had literally just been in one of them yesterday (there are two), thinking, "man, I bet this is the chore they give people who really fuck up, or really piss someone off." And now that position and all of its splendid prestige can be mine. I did make sure to ask if this wasn't a case of someone doing a shitty job on purpose just to get out of it, and was told no, it was not, but he'd have a word with whoever was on assignment before making a final decision. So there's that.

Twin and I tired of the TR drills, still days to go.

Reuben sandwiches for lunch, if I do say they were nowhere near as good as mine, even with the fancy marble rye.

Been doing the same TR drills over and over for days now; it finally got to Jackie. So tired, frustrated, and agitated over the redundant exercises. She was taken out of class for the rest of one period. The last course of the day was cut short by an hour for... that's right, bathrooms! I did get to lead the final muster clap out and cheer with a 1, 2, 1, 2, 3 boom shaka-laka-laka-boom! Hoofucking ray. Back to the room; too wiped to try and socialize, and as it was the first full course day since I've been here that I didn't have the night class until 9:45 PM, I did some letter writing (Dad, Joe) and journal (this) and hope to do some reading. Got a nice letter from Dad; still haven't had the TV fixed, still no word on the *L.A. Times* sub. Roommate Tom hit the sack early, after bitching all day about my snoring—he's lying on his side snoring like a sick wildebeest even now—like a sow in heat.

To Tom fm Joe

Tom,

I sent your Dad a big box of clothing (he had washed while he was at your apartment when you went north) along with your laptop and a batch of your mail. Yesterday I drove back down and gathered two bags of dirty clothes that you had requested, some mail, and then went to the PO Box to grab what was there. Aside from about a pound of porn circulars, the bills have been forwarded onto your Dad. I do think that after you complete your time at the facility, you should do some serious thinking about moving closer to us. Not that I'm saying anything about Long Beach (other than that it sucks), but as a former resident it is not a place that is conductive to being sober. Then again I did move to San Francisco to get away from heroin and speed, so what the hell do I know? After all the attempts to regulate booze intake (just beer from now on, etc.) you just aren't cut out to be the artistic wino anymore. You need to dry out completely... and I don't want to be a total dick (although I am pretty good at it) but your only friends around there still party. This is not a knock on them for partying, and I know that you tried to do the sober hang out thing while they were drinking, but you can't do it with that much pressure for very long. It's not a whole lot of fun to hang out with drunks or loadies when you aren't fucked.

I certainly don't have all of the answers but I think relocation is a good idea for you. Of course I'm being selfish and trying to keep you around southern California, but I think that seriously looking into an apartment in the Highland Park area (where Clare's gallery is), Altadena, Pasadena, or even downtown Los Angeles (kind of expensive), but the train system (which you have been on) would do you some good, especially if you plan on not driving. Larry Bragg has been sober for over twenty years (booze, heroin, etc. compounded with HIV) and is still artistically productive, so it is more than possible for your lazy ass. Your paper money is being used to pay for gas and shipping... so your check is still being ignored.

Keep the letters coming, and let me know if you can get reading material or candy.

Talk to you soon.
Joe

Friday, August 10, 2012

Up before 6:00 AM; and a good start to the day, took a nice shit, went to the front desk to deliver a second maintenance request form for the television. Carl, who was filling in for Charles as night man, said he'd take a look at it as soon as Tom was up.

Tom came walking into the lobby right at that moment. I threw a load of laundry in (each room only has one laundry day per week, and rooms share days, so gotta get it done early before competition and course work starts), and we took a look at it: apparently the trick is to set it to channel three, and only use the digital receiver remote, not the TV remote, to control the thing. The analog antenna actually <u>does</u> help/work here, so while there aren't many channels, it does work. So now we have radio and television, of sorts.

The earplugs worked: I'd already had a pair which, having heard Tom's snoring while at withdrawal cabin, I started using the night he got here, but with the ones I got him from Charles yesterday, he was able to get a good night's sleep. Even helped him figure out the dryer, laundry dryer that is, which is rather fancy and hi-tech—so much so that some frustrated student sometime in the past apparently put their foot through the front window of the machine.

Got letters from Joe and Dad about ready to go. Had some tea and yogurt, looking forward to breakfast and there will be no fourth course today because of "graduation" (certificates for completion of various books/programs, diplomas for those who have completed the entire Narconon program), and no night courses. Let's go. Oh yeah, and I loaned a new student, Henry, the alarm clock admin Sam loaned me (no radio), it works, he's happy, AOK.

Got through the day alright (<u>just</u> made the mail pick-up, didn't get a permanent shift on course bathroom cleaning); last course session ended with TRO: confronting, where you just sit about three feet away from somebody and silently look them straight in the face for ... well, our record is over twenty minutes now. And it was a close one, as for part of the day I was paired up with a new student, an older gent who looks kinda like a weaker, drunk version of my father—but the better part of the PM was with twin Jackie, so instead of closing down Friday staring into the eyes of a broken down (but seemingly fairly decent and reasonable) old man, I got to look into the beautiful face of a gorgeous young woman. And then we had steak for dinner—with horseradish even!

Graduation, encouraging, seems a long way off. Got to the television before Tom did, heading off an evening of football. He grumbled and fucked off to the lounge, and I'll be watching sitcom re-runs and reading Dean Koontz (*Mr. Murder*, on loan from Abby at Treeline Treatment). May wander down through campus later to see what's shaking, see if there's a movie in the lounge or maybe some cards floating around—I don't have a deck yet, and there doesn't seem to be one in the lounge. I have seen people playing some hands of something, spades I think, so I know there are some around—looking very much forward to spreading the game with no name!

Hadn't watched TV for about ... ten days, so killed some time with *Seinfeld* and *Nikita*, then wandered to the main area for some herbal tea and an apple. Ate the apple, watching some of the kids playing cards for monopoly money. Then back—for the tube in the toilet tank that sends water into the bowl to come loose and spit water out all over the floor, but this was easily remedied, was about to hit the sack, heard what sounded like water running outside. Looked out the door, it wasn't raining, stepped out wondering if a pipe had busted somewhere (toilet incident had me thinking in that direction)—turns out it was Cory, watering a newly planted avocado tree, after 10:30 PM at night, and I gave him a bit of a start ("you scared the shit out of me!"). Maybe a bit more reading, just a bit though "lights out" is extended 'til midnight Friday and Saturday. Oh yeah, Danny says he has something "fun" planned for tomorrow; James says my tests were good, and I can get the results on break sometime; and I submitted a request form to get what I need to start a "pennytalk" account so I can start using the phones (my "ten-day blackout" period ended yesterday). Not too shabby a day...

Saturday, August 11, 2012

Yes, Saturday is a full day, courses, chores and all. One of those days that, so far, has been a near-perfect balance of frustration and depression and moments of beauty and victory.

<u>Pros</u>

As I was yesterday, I was brought up short by the sunbeams through the eucalyptus and fog. Pointed it out to another recovering alkie, she agreed it was beautiful.

Eating dinner (shrimp, fried rice, orange chicken, broccoli w/ mushrooms and red peppers) in the lobby area, looked out the window and was entranced by the perfect rainbow of color that was just... perfect: red-orange-yellow-green-blue-purple, shining through prismatically as the sprinkler played through the sunlight.

Handily won the "dictionary game" we played during the final course session: supervisor reads out a definition from the dictionary, students try to name the exact word. In this one, first to get five won (prize: two small bags of candy). 'Magnanimous in victory', I shared one out at muster. (Ironically I won on the word "fluke"!)

Had some good laughs with Jackie during sessions today; got to interact a little more with the gorgeous young Asian lady, Angela, in a good and friendly fashion.

Making friends with the big pale-golden wolfish dog, Princess I think her name is, who wanders up to the ghetto from a downhill neighbor.

<u>Cons</u>

No mail at all. I've been in detox/rehab for three weeks and haven't received a single care package. Shit, I came here w/o a single book or magazine, nowhere near enough clothes, spent the entire student A/C balance on necessities, still need many things. Haven't heard a fucking word re: *L.A. Times*, and the Target store runs have proved less than efficient. Short diagnosis: it's hard to get shit here that I was taking for granted out in the world.

Fucking Tom woke me from a rather good sleep, slamming the front door at 6:15AM.

Some moments where the fucking course work actually pissed me off, made me want to leave. Everything is geared toward the program and its own special definitions; I still fail to see how the specifics of the multiple drills all actually apply to real life and recovery.

My isolation/antisocial nature has left me overly sensitive to the proximity and behavior of others. Things people say and do, and things they just might say and do, irritate me unreasonably.

Nearing nine; as muster broke a little before 8:00 PM I put forth the option of a card game, if somebody could find some cards—Sam has a deck I believe, Angie seemed mildly intrigued, Julius learned it at Treeline Treatment, and Jackie's a game player (craps, monopoly, "apple bite")... but, I don't know, there wasn't an immediate bite, and I don't even have a fucking deck of cards yet! Looks like a no on that: went for a cuppa tea and Jackie's playing "Apple Apple", Angie's talking in the dining area w/ Mike, and Sam's "jamming" with Tom.

Sunday, August 12, 2012

The only "day off" of the week... isn't. Roll call and chore assignment at 10:00 AM yielding the information that because people had been doing such a shitty job on the chores, the cable TV in the lounge was being yanked for a week or more, until significant improvement was shown. Only been to the lounge a couple times (fucking annoying it is, watching TV in a crowd wherein someone else has the clicker), but it was nice to have the option. And even further restrictions only enhance the institutional aspect of a facility under constant supervision where rules and regulations are enforced along a rigid schedule—and the forms; you need forms for everything; student requests, maintenance requests, store orders, etc.—and the request forms I've submitted I've received no response to, the store order forms for the Target runs have both been confused.

At any rate, Tom and I did the intensive room cleaning before roll call, and when that happened I got assigned to kitchen duty –cleaned the fridge inside and out, being so thorough that while I got compliments from the IC on that area, she was also pretty much hurrying me along so sweeping and mopping could be done. A much needed shower after (first since Wednesday morning) and after lunch settled down at the patio table in the front "yard" of the residential building to condense 234 pages of course book into six pages of notes. Had just started when I was hailed from the main building—I was on kitchen duty again—the daily chore, cleaning up after lunch instead of breakfast now, on top of the white glove room cleaning and campus cleaning. So, I was late for that, and checking the schedule found my name at the top of that chart region with a line under it meaning I was the IC for that area (no mention of that previously). Started in with the crew who was already at work, and immediately saw problems. One member on assignment didn't show up at all, there were a lot of areas/spots missed, and good ole Tom just walked off the job (roommate Tom, not myself). Then everyone mysteriously disappeared while I was fetching a five-gallon water bottle for the dining area—and reporting Tom to the head IC; I can't discipline anyone, even verbally, much less hand out disciplinary "chits" for violations of core conduct, but when someone refuses to do their part and literally turns their back and walks away when asked to do something, and is even given the option of performing another task... in a word, "fuck that noise". No blowback yet, but a tally is being kept. So, I stayed another quater hour past the cleaning period to put things in order. Don't have a fucking clue as to how all of that is supposed to work, don't know all of the specifics for all of the duties... it may only have been a one-time thing... (oh yeah, one of the students who graduated Friday had a visit from his parents today, and they brought ten boxes of dim sum-style pork buns and pastries for all to share.) So, after the third round of chores, settled down and finished going through the book and making notes—hope to pass the TRs 0-4 tomorrow, and <u>move on</u>.

Finished *Mr. Murder* by Dean Koontz, far-fetched but pretty engaging. Oh yeah... ah, nothing... oh yes, a couple observations: I thought it amusing/ironic/hypocritical that Tom was one of the most vocal of those criticizing the unnamed offenders who got the cable yanked for their sloppy, lazy performance, and then turned around and did the very same thing. And it seems that there are many more young(er) people here than old, or even middle-aged. And they seem to prefer their own company, playing games and trading drug-of-choice stories with people their own age (twenties, mostly it seems).

Monday, August 13, 2012

Best day in a long time! Well, actually not so long, maybe two weeks (the marathon game w/no name day with Karen, and the magic walk we took, was the best so far this year). But still, very good! There was great, thick fog in the morning and it was nice and sunny later (but not too hot): there were breakfast burritos, fruit and Danish for breakfast; was designated IC (in charge) of the morning cleaning crew for the serving/dining/entryway area (Nicole, who I met at withdrawal cabin, Julius, who I met at Treeline Treatment, and Henry, the most recent arrival); got approval to get credit card access to establish a penny talk account for phone use and newspaper subscription—hit up the Ethics Office and Ian got me online and while the *L.A. Times* won't deliver here, the *San Francisco Chronicle* will, so I set up an eight-month subscription (don't know how long I'll be here exactly, though I'm pretty sure it ain't gonna be eight months—don't know what I'll do about the extras, but fuck it, I'll deal later). Talked to James about the IQ and other tests taken when I arrived at Oakview, and he gave me my IQ score: 134; 100-110 is average. Smaller than the 167 I tested at as a child, but I think that one was flawed anyway. The others, well there isn't really any set scale I guess, so I'll be taking them all again after the sauna program and we'll all be able to see if there was any noticeable improvement: there were sloppy joes for lunch; I found a phone message from Celia, from a little over a week ago, in what people call the "email inbox", which is where I now know that they also put form approvals; got a "care" package from Dad with books, clothes, toiletries, and a letter indicating he's taking care of business (and a note from an inmate in Utah State prison inquiring about *Planarian Liberation Army*, forwarded from the PO Box by Joe).

Jackie and I passed TRs 0 (all three of those), 1, 2, 2.5, 3, and 4, after drilling them all week, so we can now start the "uppers", TRs 6-9, which shouldn't even take this full week; and at muster I received my "clear body, clear mind" certificate and recognized Jackie to the assembled group as my "awesome twin" and remarked upon the fact that we passed those hurdles and were going to be hitting the sauna, baby!

Tuesday, August 14, 2012

Not as grand a day as yesterday, but not too terribly bad. Usual routine. Started the "uppers" today, training routines 6-9 from Book 1, and got through them all a couple times, with much direction from the supe. I got frustrated more than once, but, as with the previous routines, they get a little clearer each time. Had a word or two with a rather mouthy self-righteous speed freak over my use of the word "Goddamn" ("Don't curse God's name!" "Mind your business." "It is my business!" "Then leave the room.") But it didn't lead to anything. Got a nice letter from Margaret, with a card as well, and a card from L.B. neighbor Jenny. So, cheers.

Nothing much else to report. Oh there were a couple things; the supe, Danny, took me aside, wanted to let me know that I was doing a good job, catching on well, and assured me that if he seemed exacting it wasn't because we weren't doing good work, it was just that he wanted us to start out on a good foot so we could master the TRs quickly and move on to the sauna program. And, apparently, I'm as good a "coach" as I am a "student". Getting the hang of being IC of the morning dining/serving cleaning crew. And a "funny" thing happened in course, on my way out of my chair to go out and hit the restroom, I realized my left foot was fully asleep, fully numb, from the way I'd crossed one leg over the other. When I realized, in motion, that I actually couldn't walk, I tried to make it back to my chair but my foot buckled under me and I fell on my ass, hitting the wall on the way down—there was a moment of surprised silence, until I say "damn!" and started laughing. That got some more laughter and smartass comments, which I only encouraged by doing the same. No lasting injuries so far, though, so AOK.

Thursday, August 16, 2012

Up 6:30 AM, still in a less-than-pleasant frame of mind. Finished the letter to Margaret, again got nice and sweaty before course w/the dining/service area chores. Did get to the paper before anyone else did (arrived 7:30 AM). And, after the moral decay of yesterday, we passed the more physical and direct control TRs, 6 (I&II), 7, 8, & 9—the uppers. Got "attested". Then lunch and free time until sauna calls. Gave Dean Koontz novel *Winter Moon* to one of the counselors to return to the withdrawal cabin (without ever actually checking it out officially). Like his *Mr. Murder*, it was well written and engaging, but also with a rather improbable conclusion. Trudged off to course, where Jackie and I blew through the final TRs in first period, w/ time to complete the "win" sheets, attest to the completion of Book 1, and fill out a "success story" form, and get let out before lunch. After lunch, free time for most of the day, as sauna is next and Andy said interview/orientation won't happen until tomorrow. Taught Jackie the Game with No Name; she won two, I won two. After dinner there was a "white glove" cleaning of the course rooms—I showed up, but because I was now officially on sauna time I wasn't supposed to. Stayed to offer a hand anyway (brownie points). Dusted, wiped tables, straightened books. Angie said she and Tawry (?) wanted to learn the Game, she'd come by later... didn't. Readjusted the TV antenna. Got twenty percent better reception on TV, watched some sitcoms, then a Rock Center investigative news show that featured... scandals at Narconon Centers, particularly the Arrowhead facility in Oklahoma, where three students died in nine months, and it was alleged sex was traded for drugs... Woke up to piss around 1:30 AM, saw something in the drain in the sink, looked closer, squinting, it jumped straight up in the air—it was a small frog, body about the size of my thumb. Got a couple Styrofoam cups, scooped it up, put it outside.

Oh yeah, got a "care" package from Joe—no Bermuda swim shorts, boots, or checkbook, all things I asked for, all things I need. Called him later to say thanks, conversation cut very short by the twat starting a session in the phone area/sunroom. The signs saying "session in progress" are <u>always</u> up, with no times posted, making it frustrating and annoying. And, <u>AND,</u> the cunts confiscated/put into safekeeping a postcard Joe forwarded from Kobb in Florida—it was a vintage erotic postcard showing a lady's tits—contraband! I'm beginning to distinctly dislike this place...

Friday, August 17, 2012

Dicking around in the morning, then was collected by Andy for pre-sauna paperwork. Completed that, fucked off until after lunch, spent four hours in sauna area: exercise for twenty-five minutes, alternating then twenty minutes in the sauna, sweating, with five minutes break. Vitamins, including niacin, oils, minerals, "cal-mag" (calcium/magnesium/vinegar) as additives, plus vegetables. Dinner, then graduation (got my Book 1 certification of completion), then cleaning the sauna/laundry area.

Because the sauna program schedule interferes with the regular schedule there are both perks and shortfalls: no "daily chore", no "white glove" on Sunday (campus) or Thursday (course room). <u>But</u> sauna area cleanup every day, and mail delivery is interrupted—you can't leave the sauna area for that, if your sauna period is going on between 3:00 and 3:30, you need to go in at 7:30-8:00 to pick up letters or packages, and although any usual sauna schedule will apparently be 9:00 AM to 2:00 PM, today was different. So, I went to the front desk at 7:30 PM—I had a package there, but could not retrieve it until an Ethics Officer was present to check it for "contraband". Came back a couple more times, still no show by customs.

Around 8:00 PM reception called someone and got the word that because graduation ran a little long (four graduates) there would be nobody there to examine it this evening. Thank you very goddamn much. And it was <u>right there</u>. Watched a speed eating contest (steak and pizza, left over from dinner and lunch, respectively), a game of spades, which I may have to learn how to play; and a little TV. And passed out just after 11:00 PM. Was going to... but...

Oh yeah, got two loads of laundry done as well. Very, very tired.

Saturday, August 18, 2012

Up... coffee... A call to Wells Fargo bank to get my ATM card replaced; also talked to some cat in TX re "line of credit"... not particularly helpful. Breakfast, exercise and sauna at 9:00 (actually 9:15, which was when the supervisor showed) in and out, learned to play pentagon, a Swedish version of "go". Lunch break for burgers, done by 1:30 PM. What else happened... not very fucking much. <u>Except</u>—did get a really, really nice 9 lb package of snacks and treats from the Popcorn Factory, sent by Margaret.

    peanut brittle popcorn
    caramel popcorn
    chocolate chip cookies
    gummy bears
    double twist caramels
    cinnamon popcorn
    butter popcorn x 2
    assorted jelly belly beans
    chocolate popcorn
    super sour stars
    white cheddar popcorn

buffalo ranch popcorn
kettle corn
tootsie roll midgets
jalapeno popcorn
red twists (licorice)
honey roasted peanuts
cheese popcorn x 2
salsa
Utz yellow corn tortilla chips
cracked pepper and sea salt popcorn

25 items! <u>Thank</u> you Margaret!

And a letter from Dad w/ a couple pieces of mail forwarded (bank statement, Legal Shield bill; I don't know whether I'll pay or not).

To Margaret fm Tom

Dear Margaret,

Hello! And many thanks for the massive care package! (good timing on that as well—I won a couple rounds of "the dictionary game" and the prizes were candy, and I'd been rationing the skittles but I shared out all the sour patch pieces). Oh, the dictionary game: in a rare attempt to keep the monkeys enthused, the supervisor will break during the day's courses (occasionally—very occasionally) and read a definition from the dictionary; the first person to name the word it goes with gets a point, brightened my day. Am hording it all at the moment, but if I can get some card games going (the game with no name!) I'm definitely busting some out. And popcorn in bed with one of two or three lousy channels we're blessed enough to have, winds up the day nicely.

Shit still the same here, in sauna now, so that's a five to six hour chunk of the day added to (diminished) course work and chores. And while some might fantasize about spending hours in a small box with a number of sweaty half-naked young men, well, it's not really my thing. They even separate the girls from the boys, for fuxake! Ah well, it's supposed to do wonders for mental clarity, repair damage incurred over years of substance abuse and exposure to environmental pollutants, etc.

My attitude still rather lousy at his point, admittedly, but then it wasn't real great on the outside either. Time will tell... something. "Dot. Dot. Dot." Am taking up smoking again, as gum, candy, toothpicks, and biting my tongue in impotent frustration don't always cut it.

Um, something positive, something positive... learned how to play the board/puzzle game Pentago in sauna. Dad sent The Blind Assassin *by Margaret Atwood which is turning out fairly grand; and I was able to escape the roommate's snoring and farting in his sleep to come to the dining room and work on letters relatively unmolested for an hour or so... Whups! Spoke too soon...*

So, there's the "whinge, whinge, fackin' whinge" for the day. I've got a full one ahead as I'm sure you have as well. My thanks again, and,

Love,
Tom

To Tom fm Dad

Howdy Thomas,

Much the same here—long dry spell for Portland. Your grandmother Crites has been hospitalized—will be there about two weeks while they stabilize her meds and get her nutrition squared away—then she'll go into an Alzheimer's unit at a nursing home for the rest of whenever. She's pretty violent about it, but Dad can no longer take care of her and the Social Services people stepped in.

Here's a bit of mail—I held off thinking there'd be a bigger pile from Joe, but perhaps tomorrow.

Haven't heard anything from the staff down there. Armand was really good about updates, but Lisa only calls when they want money.

I quit drinking when you went into detox. Wasn't that much, but I sure miss the glass of wine before dinner. Can't imagine what you've had to go through.

Margaret mentioned that you are doing a lot of class work and the facility info sheet mentions a lot of saunas—hope all is going well.

Love,
Dad

Sunday, August 19, 2012

It's like this—up between 6 to 6:30 AM as usual. A bit of coffee, nab the paper (Sunday edition!) before anybody else does, get breakfast, then be at the sauna area by 9:00 AM. There until 2:00 PM today. Started reading a Patricia Cornwell novel (*Trace*?). Played some pegago with Trevor and John, won a few, lost a few. When the goddamn three pages of forms had been completed, went back to the room and spent an hour cleaning the bathroom. Showered, had a couple minutes to do Sudoku/ crossword before dinner. Now it's fucking 7:00 PM and already sliding into the realm of depression and fatigue. Probably hiding out in the room for the evening, feeling, as always, alone in the crowd—not meshing with anyone in particular. Still very frustrated over my inability to get what I want/need, in general and just day-to-day, exacerbated by the lack of freedom and emphasis on schedule and control.

Wednesday, August 22, 2012

Shit, I don't know...

tom crites

To Dad fm Tom

Dear Dad,

Well, I've been "in treatment" for over two months now, and aside from the detoxing at Treeline Treatment, and the subsequent sobriety, I can't say I care for it much, in fact I'm coming to dislike it immensely. (And while the sobriety is healthy, I'm sure, and I really don't want to drink, I now regularly find myself yearning for stronger stuff.)

I entered the program with a positive mind set, in good spirits and with the best of intentions; yet every day it all seems just a bigger load of shit, the endless regimen of rules, chores, regulations, restrictions, courses, meetings, interviews, forms, questions, schedules that somehow manage to be both rigid and constantly changing at the same time, and contradictory instructions all have me turning in at "lights out" in a state of fatigued depression.

I cannot trust the staff or their agenda and somebody is always watching, listening, and stopping by "just to check" on you—maybe that sounds paranoid, but it is true that the students are always being observed and monitored, and not just by the multiple surveillance cameras around the facility; I haven't really been able to connect with anybody here (most of the students here are in their twenties and many of the students and staff are incredibly lazy, hypocritical, undisciplined, judgmental, immature, condescending—me, I'm just a prick, but at least I'm trying here); I have no access to good music, good movies or good books (although Atwood's <u>Blind Assassin</u> is turning out rather well, my thanks again for that); it is next to impossible to get the simple little things that one might want or need on a daily basis; my roommate is a swine; and I could go on and on.

Every day provides new frustration, and although I've earned three certificates for courses completed so far and was designated IC ("in charge") of one of the main cleaning shifts, these are things which will be of absolutely zero benefit when I return to the world and again face an absolute absence of prospects, except for debt, isolation and anxiety, and a view of the alley.

Perhaps this will change; I am currently in the sauna program, which over the course of a few weeks of exercise, sweating, vitamins, minerals, and other supplements is supposed to rid the body of toxic deposits that lodge within the tissues and continue to degrade physical and mental performance. But so far it's just a lot of time in a small hot box with a bunch of sweaty half-naked guys. And while my chess game has improved slightly, I'm too old for the locker room mentality and conversation that picks up regularly.

They do make escape difficult here, as aside from the surveillance mentioned earlier, all ID, cash, and credit cards are removed and placed in "safekeeping." And the only person I know in Santa Cruz, nearby, can't be bothered, so I'm here for now. But if I should fall out of contact completely, it may well be because I've told the staff exactly how I feel and where to go, and I may have been removed for proper conditioning or even "disappeared" altogether. (For more of the multi-faceted wonders of Narconon you might want to run a search for their Arrowhead, Oklahoma, facility.)

On the small plus side, Margaret has been very kind and supportive of the rehabilitation effort (and I believe she shares your view on the grandparents' situation), as has Joe (although I still need a number of items from the apt. which I sent a letter about again just recently—I did tell him where the items were and where the very "petty cash" I kept at home was, for postage and mileage). Even the neighbor, Jenny, had a good word or two, as I'd dropped her a line to let her know that if she didn't see me around for a few months it was because I was here, not lying on the floor somewhere drawing flies. And they are constantly eclipsed by the bullshit and the grind.

That's more than enough for now. I hope all's stable and well up your way, love to Linda and Rhys.

Love,
Tom

P.S. As I may have mentioned, I'd misplaced my ATM card before leaving Long Beach; I have had this cancelled and requested a replacement. When this arrives and is forwarded to you, please write to let me know, then call the number provided and have the card activated once I give you the PIN (I was going to ask you to send it here, but it will just get dumped into safekeeping; all mail is opened and searched for "contraband"–God damn I hate this.)

Thursday, August 23, 2012

Finished off the letter I started composing days ago, to Dad, bitching and griping about my current lot and listing a number of this program's failings. I had two drafts before I got one to send out, and I'm sure it sounded whinny but goddamn if I don't mean it. If they are opening the mail and reading it before it goes out, I'm fucked–like I said in it, I may get "disappeared". So, more sauna, getting the niacin (B vitamin, to break down drug deposits) booster, so should have more reactions than just a flushed face during exercise. Started the "manners" course after. No mail today, tacos for lunch though. Evening cleaning shift, drag. Short break, "white glove" cleaning of sauna area. Tired, lonely—may have to talk to someone about the fatigue and depression, <u>but</u> just don't trust them enough or find them capable enough...

To Tom fm Dad

Hi Tom,

Sorry to hear life there has become a bit unpleasant. The weekend I was there in Long Beach with you, I had three references for treatment programs: one was an AA program run by the city, but I knew you weren't keen on AA and the city offices were closed when I called Saturday after you had said you were willing to try something different. One program was in north L.A., but when I called, they had no openings for several weeks/months and I didn't think you had that much time in the shape you were in. So I was delighted to get you in at Oakview.

I don't know much about their treatment program, but I know what you've tried in the past didn't work, so what the hell, give it a shot. You've gotten sober several times and as horrific as that must be, that seems to be the easy part. The more difficult part is what this program is supposed to work on. I'm sure you are not being paranoid and that surveillance is constant, as it now is in nearly all working life. If you work in a filling station or a bank, you are under constant surveillance, a cop and a bank employee are always on camera, and it's the way we live now. Since they have to deal with druggies/ex-addicts, I'm sure that constant oversight is just part of their life and program.

Your complaint against the younger students is one every generation since before the Greeks has felt. They all are incredibly lazy, hypocritical, undisciplined, judgmental, immature, etc. and they get worse every year, I know since I've been watching for more years than you. But, we were that generation once and they will run the world next, so we just have to accept and enjoy their show. I find there's nothing I can teach them (they know everything anyway) so I've given up trying.

Talked to Lisa about future job prospects and was told they don't have a job placement function. But several "graduates" of the program work there, and sitting drunk in front of a TV wasn't landing you a lot of job offers, so maybe something will turn up. You are highly intelligent and I'm sure if you focus on it you can make more money than the general herd.

I would encourage you to share your concerns with the staff there. You are smart enough to make your case clearly and they have probably faced similar concerns in the past and should be able to explain/defend their practices. You may also be going through something like the seven stages of grief. You were happy with the detox element, a bit of question with the initial introduction, now angry at this phase of the program, you may well go through several additional emotional phases. It's got to be difficult not being able to control your own life, but I'm betting on your coming out of this just fine. In fact I'm betting everything I have, having emptied all my bank accounts, maxed out my credit cards, borrowed money from Linda and am in the process of taking out a loan on the house. I'm all in on this round, looking for you to come out strong.

Love,
Dad

Friday, August 24, 2012

Up shortly after six to run laundry, coffee, breakfast (eggs benedict!), exercise, sauna, vitamin regimen, shower. Mail, letter from Dad. More "manners". Dinner (steak and lamb chops, breaded shrimp, twice baked potatoes—not bad). Hurried to clean up before graduation. Then clean up of sauna area. Now "free time" for four hours before the extended weekend "lights out" time of midnight. (Although I'll probably turn in—11:00 PM due to the tiredness and need to keep it regular.) Nothing on TV; don't want to hang out in the lounge and watch someone else's channel surfing: fun and games—don't really want to do anything. Took some vitamins and minerals and supplements (zinc and vitamin C, feverfew, Echinacea) today, as the weather was cold and foggy through the night and Tom left the windows open—and getting out of 150° sauna, heating up again caused a few chills throughout the day and some coughing and sneezing. So, some newspaper puzzles, some reading, maybe see what's on TV later... Big Fun.

Thinking about NARCONON... there was a program on television a while ago, Rock Center on NBC, Thursday August 16. They were talking about recent deaths at Narconon's "flagship" facility in Arrowhead, Oklahoma—three in one year, specifically. Apparently over the Center's history there have been more: several were overdoses, Narconon spokesperson claimed that this was due to "students" leaving campus and smuggling drugs back into the facility, and overdosing on their own. However at least one former staff member claimed that in more than one instance staff members had given drugs to female students in exchange for sex: staff has access to patient files, and extensive interviews and urine tests would indicate which were the drugs of choice for any particular person. It would be easy to find out what any given desirable patient would be most susceptible to...

Of course this kind of thing comes up with any organization/religion/school, but it does make one think.

The very next day there was an unscheduled muster for the group wherein staff members conducted some damage control. Discounting the report entirely and emphasizing the fact that the facilities in question had helped thousands of people get clean.

About this time the cable TV in the lounge was temporarily disconnected—the reason given was that daily chores had been sloppily performed, and until this improved the cable would remain out. It was not stated which area, shift, group, or IC was responsible. This lasted for about a week. Just recently somebody mentioned that this might not have been a coincidence, rather an excuse for a "media blackout" to prevent any of this information from reaching the student body.

Suspicious. And of course all hearsay, and therefore as easily discounted as believed.

Does kind of fit in though with the fact that the program doesn't seem at all geared toward actually allowing you to learn anything, instead they'd just rather teach you to think along their lines of thought, adhering to their "definitions," toeing their line. And paying more along these lines later, I'm sure.

tom crites

To Tom fm Dad

Hello Thomas,

I followed up on your recommendation to check out the Narconon Arrowhead, Oklahoma, facility. It looks like a well-run place; fully accredited, inspected, licensed, etc. Yes, some patients/inmates/ students have died there. People die in triathlons too. My guess would be that a lot more addicts die without treatment than die in treatment. Better to die trying, than just sitting in a chair starving to death or falling down yet another flight of stairs.

I've re-read your letter and am concerned at what seems to be a pattern. You have left several positions/places angry. This is a place to deal with that and there are people there who are being paid to face that anger. Don't hold back, but learn how to deal with your immediate situation and those situations from the past that have made you walk out.

And as far as having a swine for a roommate, ask Joe what he thinks of your living conditions after cleaning out your place a couple times. We all need a little slack now and then.

Love,
Dad

Saturday, August 25, 2012

Another long, non-stop fucking day. Up, breakfast, (had some wild dreams: one horny shower scenario, another one in which I was a bounty hunter after a most wanted type by the name of something like William "Rob" Warren—found a group of his "known associates" and was interviewing them, getting the impression he wouldn't be taken alive, when I realized I was in a room full of known criminals and I didn't have a gun...) Exercise, sauna, shower, no mail, course, dinner, IC of service/

dining, sauna cleaning, course again, finished Manners course, attested it, then TV.

"It doesn't matter whether the glass is half-full of half-empty; what matters is (that) you have the glass."

To Tom fm Margaret

Dear Tom:

Good to hear from you again. I hope you received the care package. Dad said you don't have a sweet tooth, and I knew you like savory/spicy things. But, then in your last letter you said that your tastes for sweets has returned. I hope there was enough for you to host some friends and/or bribe others. I figure that in the world of rehab, snack food might be the currency of choice.

Named "in charge" huh? Is this because of your outstanding performance or were they thinking that some leadership and responsibility might make you buy in more? Or a bit of both? So, does this mean you are ultimately responsible for it getting done, or you get to supervise others? I would imagine that getting others, especially people who are at varying degrees of willingness to be in rehab, to work towards a common goal might be a frustration all in and of itself.

Back when I was a teen, after a suicide attempt, my school counselor gave me IQ tests. The depression/trauma/distraction translated into a few lost points too. Of course, it didn't help much that I spent about as much time telling him what I thought was wrong with his testing methodology as actually answering the questions. I imagine that your nutritional intake wasn't optimal before going into rehab. I've learned from my eating disordered clients that the brain really does need a decent caloric and nutritional intake to be fully functional. Perhaps when you get your body healthier, your points will return.

I have the third Dragon Tattoo book, if you'd like me to send it to you. It is a little different than the first two books, in that it very much centers around the conspiracy and court case. But, it does make for a good resolution to the story. I've got some crime dramas I could cull from the shelves too, if you'd like.

We had a hell of a week/weekend with my work last week. We had six ER calls. There are agencies in our state that don't take six ER calls in a year. (My agency provides information/assistance/ support to victims while they undergo evidence gathering/medical treatment after an assault/rape.) Over the weekend, we had four calls alone. Which, I think, may be a record for a weekend. But, one of the things I love about this work is that I often can be the link between various police/court departments. One of our victims was a fourteen-year-old girl who was raped by a thirty-seven-year-old cousin. In the course of talking with the victim and her family, they mentioned that the thirty-seven-year-old was involved in an ongoing custody battle for his five-year-old child. The mother of the child was trying to keep him from having any visitation. Just in passing, they mentioned that she was really young and that they assumed her parents were behind the custody issues because they hated the guy. One of the detectives in that department is someone I've worked with a lot... I mentioned this to her, and she looked up the mother's age. And found that she was only fifteen when she had the baby and he was thirty-two, which is statutory rape. No wonder she didn't want him to have access to her young daughter. Now, he's facing charges for raping two underage girls, and she has instantly won her custody case. Because she never reported it as rape/inappropriate relationship, the family courts didn't bother to look at the age issues. Makes me look like a flippin' genius.

Bruce started back to school late last week. And, over the weekend, we got our first "dude slipped a mickey into a girl's drink and raped her" case of the school year. I think the guys had it set up. She said that every single guy at the party introduced himself with either initials or crazy nicknames. And, research shows that more often than not, college guys actually work in concert to assist each other in raping girls. Assholes.

Granny has been in the hospital for the past couple of weeks to get her into some sort of shape to go into long-term care. Cathy called this evening and said that Granny has stopped eating. The social worker says she believes Granny has given up. Three years ago when all this started and she still had some functioning, she did tell me that she was ready to die. And, I think if she had known five years ago that she would end up in this shape, she would have killed herself. She is being moved to a long-term care facility on Monday. They don't expect she will live very long. Granddaddy has said that he plans to move to Missouri in November and buy himself a flat screen TV. Nutball.

You said that the next phase of your treatment can bring back flashbacks and bring to the surface all sorts of crap stored in your system. I'm sure it could be disincentive to continue if it's too icky. But, if you can get through the icky stuff, perhaps you can let go of it forever. Feel free to rant and rave to me if you need to, I understand the source.

Love you.
Margaret

Sunday, August 26, 2012

Day of rest—again, not so much. Sauna started at around 160° today, and there were eight guys in ours, including two who were at least 100 pounds overweight. Roommate's malodorous feet. Bad music on the iPods. Not great. Some shit coward comments from cunts on the volleyball court during piss commute. Chores (washing windows). Room cleaning (didn't have the bathroom portion this week). In the morning Henry presented me with a pack of Camel Blue (my brand) as a token of appreciation for giving him the sports and business sections of the *S.F. Chronicle* in the mornings, so I won't have to beg 'em for a day or two. Kinda tense and shitty, but after the chores were over, Maureen showed me where to pick fresh rosemary. Somebody left a 600 puzzle Sudoku book out for the working, and I found the best place to look out down into and across the valley to the sunset. Now *X-men: the Last Stand* is on, I've got Margaret's popcorn, roommate is out playing in the Oakview limp rockers, and I have some small amount of precious privacy and peace and quiet. Ahhh...

Monday, August 27, 2012

One of the first things I saw this morning was that wonder of nature, two snails fucking. (or at least preparing to fuck—"face" to "face," mouths and feelers reaching into each other's shells.) Wondered if that would be a good omen: didn't really turn out to be, the day none too sterling. Up to nine people in sauna, very unpleasant—I was actually mentally composing a formal letter of complaint to Ethics for a good part of the day. Got a weird twinge in the back hauling a five-gallon water bottle out of the rack, but got some feverfew (sp?) and a cold pack to prevent swelling and hopefully any pain next day (it worked)—but not before I finished restocking the water, doing the dining room chore, and the sauna. Campus-wide muster later, a number of new people down from withdrawal. Crap, though it seems that the number of people just "leaving" the program for reasons that aren't made publically clear, combined with the number of "retreads," people who've been through the program before, relapsed, and returned, outnumber easily the number of people who graduate each week. Did get my "drugs: how they affect your body, your mind, and you" course and "manners course" certificates... both of which will serve me so well in the next life. There may have been some other shit too...

Tuesday, August 28, 2012

Sauna a little better today—one guy "passed" the course and another candied out and went back to his room (or had an extreme reaction, either way he made space and nobody missed him) so there was not such the oppressive sardine atmosphere. More "Beginning Health" course, hauled and restocked about ten five-gallon bottles of water, had a brief snack party with three of the guys, tired as shit.

To Margaret fm Tom

Dear Margaret,

Hello! Good to hear from you as always. Life sounds intriguing out on your side of the world—I really don't know how you deal with the horrible situations you encounter every week: that takes something. I don't know if I mentioned this before, but I really respect that. It's good to see/hear people actually working against the tide of human malevolence.

I wish I had encouraging word re the grandparents' situation, or there was something I could do. I know, full well, that everybody's time is going to come, but it's still sad to see the good lights go out. I wonder at times if I should have taken the opportunity to go out and help out as a caretaker, but they really need somebody with a driver's license (I haven't had one for over fifteen years), and like I said to Dad once, well, I just don't care for Grandfather that much. Kind of an uncharitable attitude on my part I know, but Dad understood. (Plus, I am a bit selfish/self-absorbed –I'm working on that, but I have been living alone for about fifteen years and thoughts/concerns are generally directed inward, or downward, depending on the depth of the bottle... hopefully enough of that for a while.)

Still in sauna program daily, five hours per (minus thirty *minute exercise warm-up, brief breaks and lunch). Not a complete killer, except when they pack eight-nine people in at once. No hallucinations or "realizations" yet, but we'll see. Has given me a chance to improve my chess game, and there's a Swedish marble game called Pentago that I've been enjoying, and plan to try to find a set for Dad once I get out (so don't spill the beans!). Read a couple books from the very limited "library" here while in the sweatbox, Patricia Cornwell's <u>Trace</u>, which was intriguing and well written, but with a disappointing ending, and Martin Cruz Smith's (the cat who wrote <u>Gorky Park</u>) <u>December 6</u>, which I liked very much. If you recommend the third book in the <u>Girl with the Dragon Tattoo</u> series I'd love to take a look at it. And others you might suggest—you mentioned some crime novels, those would be right up my alley. Speaking of crime novels, have you read James Elroy's <u>The Black Dahlia</u>? Excellent—so much better than the movie. Also liked Patricia Highsmith's novels that I've read—she's the lady behind <u>The Talented Mr. Ripley</u> saga, and her short story anthology <u>Eleven</u> is awesome—not one, but <u>two</u> stories of killer snails!*

Still very much enjoying the Popcorn Factory goodies, rationing some, sharing some out, all good. For some reason the facility doesn't receive a newspaper, but after multiple forms I managed to get the <u>S.F. Chronicle</u> delivered here (again, can't remember what I've relayed already) and have been trading the sports and business sections for cigarettes, so free trade, of a sort, is alive and almost well.

Seeing a bit in the news about N.O. flooding—they don't seem to get much of a break. Saw one poor lady on the news who'd just been flooded out of her home, which was destroyed, for the third time...

I don't know if you had ever mentioned a suicide attempt to me before—if you did, please forgive me, I am admittedly ignorant and self-absorbed at times. But without a doubt the world is a better place with you here. So needless to say, I'm glad that you're here too. Sent a bit of a rant to Dad about the conditions here, admittedly a bit childish, but then they treat addicts like children here so I didn't think it too far out of line (I did rewrite it several times, but kept coming to the same points, so...). Got a letter back from him today, in which he addressed some of my complaints, had some points and suggestions, and closed with a summary of how far out on a limb he had to go to get treatment for me. I did see how much a large part of it cost on one of the admission forms, and I never would have considered a program of that magnitude. He's already done more than could be expected, as have a few of my close friends. My attitude towards the program and the future is still bad, but, as I recognize it I will try to improve it and move forward instead of grinding away in reverse.

Hope your fall season is a fine one, and,

Love,
Tom

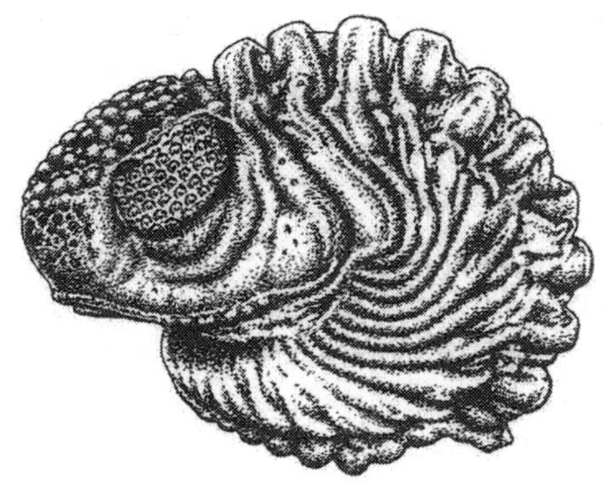

Phacops africanus
(enrolled)

Prehab 2009

Spring, 2009

So, I figure I have about two years. Two years of freedom, without a boss, without a schedule. I have $63K in the bank, and living modestly at $2K/month that gives me little room for error or extravagance, barring fatal accident or illness. I haven't worked in six months, since leaving the bank and do not plan to work again. I could reconcile myself to the fact that I was spending the majority of my waking hours making money for somebody else, but I am no longer willing to work so hard to be so unhappy. To work ceaselessly for no real reward, surrounded, at work and away, by the same people, who, no matter where they live or what they do, continue to demonstrate the same willful ignorance and blind arrogance that allows them to act as if each one of them is the only person on the planet.

I'm tired of it. I'm tired of it all, of everything. I'm tired of the demands made simply to stay alive, tired of being alone as a constant outsider despite not being able to stand others' company, tired of proving myself to no point, tired of trying new things, tired of trying. I may not make it two years. I may hang it up before then.

"and now I am master of myself"—Cato

"to be or not to be; that is the question."—Hamlet

One month sober today. Thirty days ago I woke up after binge drinking for two-and-a-half weeks to find myself totally fucked. I'd been feeling kind of shitty for a few days, what with the constant drinking, eating shitty canned or frozen food when I'd eat anything at all, and not drinking nearly enough water. But I just drank through it. So, it caught up with me, and I found myself, as I say, totally fucked. I was actually bloated, and it felt like my organs were all swollen and grinding against each other. Everything in my back hurt as well; spine, muscles, organs, it was bad enough that every time I took a breath it would cause a muscle spasm in my back which would in turn cause my diaphragm, which felt like it had actually been pushed up higher in my chest due to the swelling, to contract, constricting all of my guts into a painful ball of shit; lying in any position other than flat on my back made it feel like things were sliding painfully out of place, I was also severely dehydrated; my lips were peeling badly and my piss was orange, what little of it there was.

Unfortunately I couldn't even keep water down, so I couldn't rehydrate, couldn't eat any aspirin, and certainly couldn't drink. All I could do was lie on the floor (a friend told me that for a bad back a good remedy was to sleep/lie on a hard floor instead of a soft bed), waiting for something to pop and trying not to breath too deeply.

Over the next couple days I was able to get some Tums and Pedialyte and start rehydrating, but it was about four days before I could eat solid food and a week before my piss was clear.

So, now I have a lot more time. Time that I used to spend drinking. Reading more. Eating much better, exercising more. Shorter on patience and tolerance; can't wash away irritation with a six-pack anymore. I get tired of being conscious all the time, though.

Wanted to get out of the apartment and get some movie popcorn butter, so went to check out the new Kevin Smith flick _Not so good Buddy!_ Kinda rude and amusing in places, but basically a movie about a porno that turned into a chick flick. Had hoped at the very least to write it off as research for _Adult Film School_, but no such luck. The only inspiration to be found was the lesson not to turn the story into a weepy piece of shit and forget about finishing the porno in the end. But it did have some cute chicks...

Building yard sale. "Worked" from 7:00 AM to 11:00 AM, sold $5.00 worth of DVDs, gave away two CDs, three beers.

Neighbor who had been planning the event for weeks, including getting permit ($200 fine without!) and advertising, ended up putting most of their shit out for "donation" by the dumpster due to poor showing. Enflamed the liberal ire of a couple neighbors by suggesting upside-down exclamation points be added to the purple-spraypaint-on-bedsheet sign advertising "Yard Sale! Today!" in order to attract Hispanics. Don't know why... oh yeah—liberals!

Still getting anxiety attacks, and using pot and alcohol to combat them, but so far not such a bad year. I do keep stealing peoples' lighters though... Went over to Celia's later to vacuum out her fireplace. Bill was over drinking, and I eventually got loaded enough I needed a couple hints to leave C. alone with her cold. But she was appreciative, and as it's midwinter, a place with a fireplace is good to know.

Dream:

Traveled to an inside location, a workshop/studio/gallery that also served as an art library—rows of shelves at chest height filled with books, phonebook-sized full-color catalogs propped open on top. Shopping for something, met an Asian businessman who sold me the most amazing artifact: a lantern sized gemstone of translucent green, with a perfect semi-human figure carved inside. Figure was crouching, and of ambiguous sexuality, calling to mind a mermaid/angel. The color of the stone made the figure look as if it were in an ocean of some misty miasma. Figure all green except for an upraised head, which was of brilliant reddish pink. Detail so smooth, clear and perfect it seemed to have a fourth-dimensional glow. Topping the item was an immense raw opal, crude and unpolished but carved with almost Marquesan designs through which you could see the depths of color and flaws of the gemstone through the dark outer stony surface, Cost: $225,000.00. Packing up to leave, I could not fit all of my art supplies and belongings into my moving box.

Got up and went downtown to get cash as early as possible, 6 AM. Of course came back in a foul mood. It wasn't even the beggars this time—it was the fucking dog walkers. Tourist staying in the Ocean Boulevard hotels with their fucking dogs. Taking them on their little walks and literally filling the air with the smell of fresh dog shit, ruining the perfectly good morning air, and I mean there were a lot of the cunts. You've got to have some sort of mental disorder to depend on a lower animal for love and companionship, unless you live in the fucking Yukon. And to take the beast traveling with you...

Needed a paper, but all along Ocean the boxes for the *Press-Telegram* were empty but for signs saying that papers were no longer being delivered at that location. The busiest street in Long Beach...

Hit Kinkos after the grocery store, and realized my backpack has just about had it. Fucking Jansport and their niggardly design flaws—the borders of the zipper halves are too wide and the excess is left hanging for the zippers to catch on when zipped. This tears up the bag and throws zippers out of alignment. This is the second Jansport backpack I've had with the same problem. Goddamn but I'm a grumpy old fuck at middle age.

Yesterday I decided first of the month I'll have been sober long enough. Months without getting high and six weeks without drinking. Come the first I am getting fucked up. For about a week. Oh yeah, and I'm tired of the side effect of this healthy fucking high-fiber diet. This is the second time this week I've plugged the toilet. And a few days ago one of those logs literally ripped my ass. My ass!

Ha! Fuck the first: broke out the bag and a bottle of wine on Friday night and had a nice and toasty evening. "Here's to five long weeks on the wagon, and the irreparable harm that it's caused me!" But I did learn two things about sobriety:

1. Sobriety is tiring. I had the feeling that I was running around "doing things" all the time. Couldn't even sit still for the duration of a movie.

2. I am a much bigger prick when sober. I'm an uptight grumpy fuck at the best of times, but when sober I <u>always</u> seemed to be pissed off.

Spent the day socializing. Went by the dealer's and picked up a bag. Split a bumper and hung out shooting the shit, playing with the dog. Then went back to Joe's to drink and smoke, and fucking Joe A. has some sort of seizure, coughing, difficulty breathing, and he goes limp and quiet, a torrent of drool falling out of his mouth. Had to pop him in the chest and call his name to get him to come around, and even then it took him several minutes to recover. Spent another three or so hours there on and off, wondering if he was going to fucking die. But he appeared to be okay when I left (9:30), having said it had happened before and wasn't a big deal—blame it on "the good shit".

Been getting very loaded very frequently lately; unhappy and agitated, very tired quite often. Still depressed and without hope; work, people, sex, money... all seems pointless, no point in writing about it either. Art and writing no longer sources of inspiration; too much effort for questionable purpose. Boo-fucking-hoo.

Woke up around 4:00 AM this morning, and once I started moving around felt surprisingly good. Drank for about eleven hours yesterday, but ate all day so there was no vomiting. Anyway, got online and started looking for sites that might help promote the artwork. Signed up with Gothic.net, then went out running errands. Picked up food and booze (supposed to be rainy for days), cash, and found a couple DVDs for review waiting for me at the Post Office. Came back home, cleared the sink of dishes and started writing the first CD review in well over a year. Even got a load of laundry in. I feel good, so something bad must be about to happen.

Feeling better, got food, water, fruit juice, bouillon, vitamins, etc. all down. Still no sleep beyond a couple hours, but hoping tonight. Finished two books, *Leaving Las Vegas* by John O'Brien and *Flesh of my Brother* by J. Allen Manis, the 1946 account of travels through cannibal-infested New Guinea. Still low points however, keep coming back to what I believe to be the central components of my unhappiness. I'm certain that it's the regimen of bullying and brutality imposed by my parents from what seems like day one. This was so regular and overdone that it seems to have destroyed any shred of self-confidence before it had a chance to develop. For fuck's sake, my adopted sister was so badly abused she had to be removed from the home and placed in foster care at age eleven or twelve. I got it too, but not nearly as bad, and at least she got away. I'll always hold resentment, and a certain degree of hate, for that childhood. Granted, it's all the responsibility of the individual at some point, but it's not unreasonable to ask for a better start.

Been a decent couple days. Yesterday went by Joe A.'s to smoke, and he completely re-did a planter Paul and Laura gave me as a housewarming gift years ago. It's a wide clay bowl that originally held three varieties of cacti, but had been somewhat, I regret to say, neglected. Joe took the tiny spiny one that looked dead and transplanted it to a chili bowl of mine, which now sits in the kitchen window hoping for resurrection. The other two he moved around, then surrounded them with about four varieties of succulents in a really beautiful arrangement. The night before I was standing at the drafting table working on a collage when Bill and Cecia came through the alley and saw me, and between shouting and throwing things got me to come out for drinks. We got smashed at Celia's, then went to the bar (Broadway) where Bill's lover works and got more smashed, Jack and Cokes, gingerbeer shots, the Cramps and the Pogues on the juke box. Went back to Celia's after, but don't remember much after that. Woke up at home, don't remember getting back there. Still getting anxiety attacks, and using pot and alcohol to combat them, but so far not such a bad year.

Lost the battle this morning. After running out of ink for the printer, fighting with Monster.com to try to get my résumé posted, then hoofing it through downtown scum to Walmart only to find they didn't have the cartridge I needed, I was once more in the grip of anxiety and depression and began morning drinking. On the plus side, I did get up early (thanks to anxiety and depression, plus a fragment of a zombie dream), got *Adult Film School* (v2.5) transferred to CD, put on the second PC and printed, hit the grocery store, worked on the résumé online, re-trimmed the haircut and cleaned all the dishes in the sink. Yesterday was much more productive, here's hoping I shake the lethargy after a good nap. The entire job/money scheme has me depressed as shit, but it still beats waking up at three or four in the morning stressing out over the pile of work I have waiting at the office and at the same time knowing, just knowing, that somebody is going to fuck things up today and I'm going to have to deal with it.

Took care of some business today: went to H&R Block and got my taxes done by a nice, if somewhat overly religious, Hispanic lady. Had them done professionally because of the taxable events last year. Cashing out the 401(K) and cash balance plan. Taxes were taken off the top, but different people had told me different things about additional fees/penalties for early withdrawal. But, according to the tax lady, I actually have $892.00 coming to me from Federal (check should be here in three to four weeks) and $54.00 from State (although California isn't paying out any time soon). Hit the Post Office and found the black ink cartridge I'd ordered (finally got it after what, a month of getting dicked around?). Installed and aligned that, did some grocery shopping, laundry, etc. Wrote a couple reviews, got a chapter done for *Adult Film School*, a couple chapters actually. I just hope H&R didn't fuck up the returns. The lady was unfamiliar with retirement plan payouts, but her supervisor confirmed the procedure. But what was really strange was that it took four people, none of whom seemed to know what they were doing, to process my fucking $168.00 check.

Not so depressed and anxious this weekend... but still filled with hate for my family: I hope we all die as slowly and painfully as Fran did, except grandmother. Some people just never should have had children. I will hate you all with all I have until the day I take my own life.

Summer, 2009

Still recovering from Monday. Ate, drank, smoked too much, vomited all day Tuesday, so much so that I threw out my back. Organs swollen and aching like the previous breakdown. Could barely move, pills didn't help. Everything hurt, nothing comfortable. Extended through Wednesday, shuffling pitifully between chair and bed, trying to sleep. Also realized a little more fully the two-faced nature of the neighbors. Absolute pieces of shit. Arrogant swine much too full of themselves. Bad fortune coming for all. At any rate, ran some errands today, finished a couple movie reviews. Able to keep solid food down, but had the shits all day. Hope to fuck I can begin drinking again tomorrow or this weekend. The hopeless reality of utter shit literally too depressing to bear. Down to $51K; no hope for anything but ruin in sight.

Sick and sleeping yesterday. Busier today. Woke up 3:00 AM, showered, washed hair, shaved for first time in days. Paid bills and wrote review of *Blackguard* while finishing *The Man Who Wasn't There*. Went out and mailed mail, picked up cash at downtown ATM, then hit grocery store for whiskey and pedialyte. Came home, napped, then did laundry while updating the Paniscus Review website. Had some watermelon and wine, then folded laundry. Hope to do some online searching and horror review writing later. Got an email from Chad Hensley, *Esoterra* magazine. Creative [Creation] Books is publishing a "Best of" collection (hardly worth it if you ask me) and he wants to use an illustration of mine that was on the cover of *Esoterra* #7. We'll see, "there will be payment," but that is still "to be determined". Cleared the sink of dishes, worked on a drawing for the first time in a long time, vacuumed the vents and filters of PS3. Father's Day this weekend, Father's birthday next week, there will be nothing from me—filled with hatred, anger and resentment, just as I was taught.

No real plans for the fourth. Went grocery shopping, picked up booze and food. Made chicken wings and carrot sticks, none too shabby. Spent a few hours helping Mr. Fowler move into a ground floor (bad knee). Lots of dust, but no cockroaches or dead rodents under the furniture. Also helped haul Johnny and Lisa's fancy new air conditioner upstairs. Went over to Joe A.'s rolled one and in a little bit Lisa came by to invite us to an impromptu barbecue at Celia's. Went over, fought the grill, had BBQ chicken and hot sausage on a roll. Went down to Shoreline Drive to see the fireworks, and it was crowded as fuck; tourist, cops, kids, etc. Fireworks of Long Beach were none too impressive, but from that close to the beach we could see those of other cities. We were hoping the blimp circling the area would get too close to the explosions and go down ("oh, the humanity!"), but no such luck. Went back to Celia's, hung out for a while and made breakfast plans. Very much in agreement we didn't plan the whole weekend around that underwhelming display.

Fall, 2009

Recovering from another alcoholic breakdown, again. Much smaller this time, I managed to avoid the vomiting but still had the pain and bloating and the bad back. Even a little blood in the stool this time, this was mostly yesterday. Spent much of the day flat on my back on the floor. Did finish a book and a half though, Michael Dibdin's *Dirty Tricks* and most of Mishima's autobiographical *Confessions of a Mask*. (Working on Ed Abbey's *Beyond the Wall* right now). Felt all of this coming on Thursday, but had been cooking Cuban black bean stew for three days and had Celia coming over for dinner that night so just drank through it. Was able to move around more today, shit, shave and shower, water plants, do some computer shit. May even be able to eat real food tonight; the stew filled my biggest pot, and even after sending a load home with Celia and giving a load to Joe I've got a ton left. Oh yeah, wrote a review of *Mystics of Bali* as well. Taking it easy tonight, staying in, TV and reading, no booze. Hopefully won't have bad night sweats, chills or dreams like last night. Still very angry most of the day, reflecting upon my life, and am still not happy with it. Tried so hard at so many things, but to no concrete end purpose. Failed due to my own weakness. Was taught weakness and failure from the start so no real surprise, but still very disappointing. Hope to resume drinking myself to death tomorrow. Things are the way they are, but not for very much longer. Oh yeah, the big toe on my left foot has gone partially numb.

A long period of ill health. Got to drinking whiskey, 75 South, with water, all day, every day. Stopped eating. Smoked a lot. Got the shakes, bad. All over. Practically an invalid some days, lay in bed sweating and shivering. So bad I could barely write out my bills. Could barely leave the home. Then I caught a cold and tried to drink through that, but it settled into my lungs. Finally had to stop drinking altogether to avoid pneumonia (severely compromised immune system at this point). First day dry a nightmare, next a little better. Much fruit, juice and vitamins. Read a lot. Watched TV, movies. Banged my foot up pretty bad, swollen and sore for a few days. Still coughing a little, but feeling much better. Writing reviews, updated the website yesterday for the first time in months.

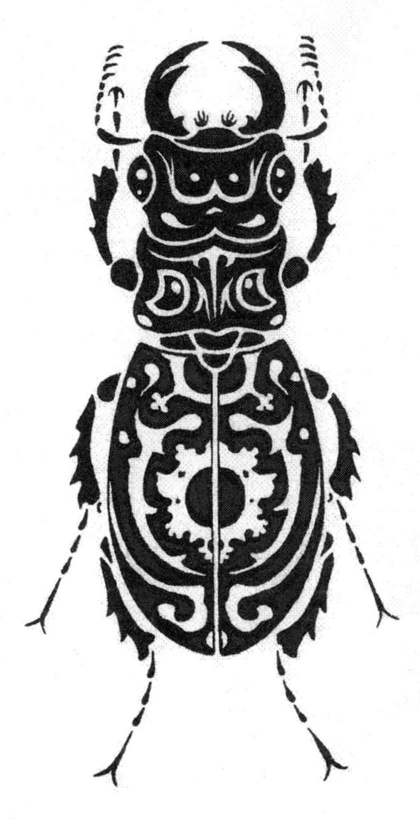

Rehab *Second Month*

Saturday, September 1, 2012

A trying few days; see letters to follow. Schedule and sauna—bitch. Humping water bottles, fractioning off the soul for cigarettes—owe Victoria nail polish and remover for a pack of Virginia Slim 120s, which was a source of great amusement for the sauna mates who saw me smoking them, and then the roommate came through with a loan, put a carton of cigarettes on his S.O.F. (requested Lava Blue, a borderline generic, got Fortuna, a borderline generic). Finished course work on "Beginning Health", started an addiction course. Had to call the *S.F. Chronicle*, didn't get the paper yesterday, and it didn't show up today by the time I was getting ready for sauna. Hump, stress, worry, shit. Moment or two of decency, but mostly the same negative attitude. No mail today, apparently the Post Office decided to make Labor Day weekend a full three day weekend.

Had a great and inspiring dream the other night: was looking through a book that was perhaps the actual *Necronomicon*—all sorts of odd alien/skeletal/ornamental objects surrounded by Arabic calligraphy, interlocking all; calligraphy forming intricate designs, pictures and emblems unto themselves. Great idea for a book project—I could put anything into the words. Need to find an Arabic/English dictionary, as well as books on Arabian calligraphy! Tomorrow: sauna, white glove room cleaning, evening chore (probably), sauna cleaning. Speaking of sauna, got the niacin dose upped, had a solid reaction—flushing and prickly heat all over (almost).

To Dad fm Tom

Hello—and thank you for your letters. I realize my last was a bit reactionary and ungrateful (not to mention hypocritical—I know I share some of the same traits I derided my fellow students for, but it's still unpleasant to see that kind of thing regularly in a confined setting), but I did rewrite the rant several times and the sentiment remained the same. I am hoping, planning rather, that this will change between now and my estimated "graduation" time of November—something. I am attempting to recognize/reconcile my disagreements with the program, although I'm still leery of speaking with staff—their pattern seems to be to take problems as signs of a "reaction" or the fact that a student just "doesn't understand" (and perhaps have them meet with a "wordclearer"). And it all goes into the big file... I do understand the surveillance aspect, and treating the students like children, to a degree, but it is definitely restricting. And the occasional grilling I've heard of, of students being interrogated about other students' activities, still seems a bit off. But all in all I'm quite sure there are worse programs.

When I considered entering treatment I had no idea it was such an immense investment. (I had no idea of anything for a long time actually. That didn't work out so well.) I really don't know what I would have said. But as I did say before, I'm here for now, and will do my best to make the best of it. The weekly graduations and completion certificate presentations are always loaded with endorsements from participants at different points in the Program, so it's apparently working for people.

Thank you, again.

Love,
Tom

To Tom fm Dad

Hi Tom,

There's no argument that your current living arrangements are not optimal. Being forced to live with someone not of your own choosing, having hours and conditions dictated by others, has got to be pretty annoying. And as your health (physical and mental) improves it will probably be even more so. On the other hand, your rent is paid and you don't have to wonder where your next meal is coming from.

Word from my parents (always indirect, never hear from them direct anymore) is not good. Mom is in supervised care and though she occasionally hits some of the staff, she's ninety years old and 80 pounds, how much damage can she do? She won't eat some times but seems in no immediate danger of dying -which is what she would prefer I'm sure. Dad is just a loose cannon. We can't control him and never know what he is doing at any given time, but seems to be going downhill pretty fast.

Weather here continues to be beautiful, shorts and t-shirts, no rain for more than a month. You can feel fall in the air, trees are starting to drop leaves, and mornings are more brisk. As I recall, weather in your area is pretty nice and uniform. Hope you have the chance to walk about in it a bit.

Take care. Love

Monday, September 3, 2012

Shit yesterday (sauna, three chores), shit today (sauna, course, two chores, muster). Getting the cold many others here have: no surprise. On top of the smoking, the roommate's got it. He leaves the fucking window open at night (after being awoken the second time this morning before 5:45 by his seeming random cursing and banging I had to ask "what the fuck is going on over there, man?". He was having a fit about the heat coming on in the morning; on top of the 120 extra pounds and the general state of ill health, the heater makes him even more uncomfortable. When I helped him pull out the bed to examine the vent under it that was causing such "problems," that he claimed could simply not be adjusted, I pulled the grate up and found it missing the shutters that would close it. I checked the other one in the room and found that not only did its shutters work, but it could be easily pried up as well. I offered the suggestion that they might simply be switched: "No, I'll just deal with it." I switched them anyway while he was at course.) And there's the sloppy factor: when he borrowed some of my mouthwash, he managed to switch caps on the bottles—now the cap from the mouth of the bottle he's been tipping his mouth to, and the cold germs it carries, is sitting on mine. Some other assorted nonsense, can't wait for more disturbed dreams of blowjobs and apartment break-ins.

Wednesday, September 5, 2012

Cold kicking in, kicking my ass for the past two days, slept for more than ten hours last night—even w/o the tried and trusted Nyquil and whiskey regimen. So, every single little thing burns with irritation. But, taking the "cold packs", zinc, vitamin C, echinacea, feverfew, that's basically what you get at Oakview. Dozed between sauna and chores, skipping dinner today as I did yesterday—hard to get the required rest on a tight schedule. Felt kinda shitty and ill-humored most of the day, but had a couple of moments. Nan asked me "wanna hang out?" as our chore paths crossed (chore right after course, etc. Wiped that one out, even if she wasn't fucking teasing with me). Nicole laughed so hard during sauna clean up she puked, and Joe called re: what he can or can't send here. Can't call back yet due to "objectives" taking place... No mail yesterday, no mail today.

Sunday, September 9, 2012

Another day of sauna—soaking in sweat, listening to bullshit talk and bullshit music, now thanks to the four new beach frat boys who just started the program. Getting easier on the system, especially now that the cold is almost beat, but the facilities, crowding, supervision (or lack thereof), on top of the five hour per day program, the impossibility of steady reading due to sweating, and the difficulty concentrating, it all has me mentally drafting a report on the program's shortcomings. Speaking of which, it's almost daily that new insidious violations of privacy by staff are brought up: from spying on students, interrogating students about other students' activities, limiting what little freedoms there are, etc. And if you ask to leave, you'll have to have police come to release your ID and cards and currency. No privacy, no security. Almost makes one paranoid... as if I didn't want to be here in the first place, every day seems to provide a good reason not to.

To Tom fm Joe

Tom,

So what's going on at your end? When I talked to you briefly a while back it sounded a little like you were calling me with an empty soup can on the end of a string. Have you made any progress toward figuring ways to sleep especially with snoring roommate situations? Your apartment still smells like the inside of a burning cigarette factory, but I have made a few half assed attempts at cleaning a bit... don't get too excited it ain't much. Still sending your bills to Dad, and checking the PO Box as well, so nothing really to worry about at this end. Can you get books or periodicals sent to you? I don't know if they frown on such things because they want you focused on what's going on or not. Comics? Novels? Boring ethnographic books? A sketchbook?

I can't say that too much has been going on around here other than Bonnie's Cthulu being removed shortly after mine. I officially moved out of storage today and have been making progress clearing out crap that I was paying rent to store. One thing that was in there (besides Japanese toys from the mid-nineties that had begun to decompose from heat) was an old fifties couch frame, which I sawed into pieces and had Ian throw into a dumpster. Aside from a carpet of mouse droppings, everything looked about the same as when I crammed most of it in there about three or four years ago. This is probably the first time we've been without a storage unit since about '98 or so. I shudder just thinking about how much money I wasted at 150 bucks a month warehousing crap for all of these years.

Talk to you soon.
Joe

Monday, September 10, 2012

Tossed and turned a bit last night, had a hard time getting back to sleep after pissing at 4:00 AM, but eventually did and woke up at 7:00 AM and felt pretty good. Newspaper already delivered, a plus, loaned Margaret Atwood's *The Blind Assassin* (which I finished last night—Dad was right, she is a "beautiful writer", so good I found myself copying out lines and passages, and most likely will read again) to Cindy at the front desk, a plus. Didn't get to start sauna until almost 9:30 AM due to supervisor timing, but had the niacin level bumped up to 2300 with minimal reaction. Started another course "Helping someone overcome addiction", got taken out for a brief ethics interview re: sauna program, life at Oakview, etc. Very diplomatic, I think, which is definitely the way to handle such. Interview went past 5:00 PM, so didn't get to serving area until 10 after, and there was still a line out the door, which would have given me about ten minutes to bolt food—skipped it. After dinner chore, sauna chore, now an hour until evening muster and certification handout. Sauna had thirteen fucking guys in there at one time—definitely anti-therapeutic, which I brought up with ethics ("good to know...").

Wednesday, September 12, 2012

Two small victories today: talked to Joe this morning, and he confirmed that he did, apparently, get the last letter I sent (so they aren't being intercepted for some reason by O.R. staff, a concern another inmate expressed yesterday). He just hasn't sent the list of things I requested from home. Can't complain, he did send a very nice hardcover *Asian Tribes* book that I plan on getting good use from. Still wondering why Karen hasn't written back after over three weeks. Maybe it was intercepted, here or there, maybe it wasn't 'appropriate', or maybe she's too busy to give the proverbial rat's ass. And today began the new shift change at the sauna. The afternoon crew not starting until 2:00 PM—which means even if the late-ass supe doesn't get his shit together until 9:30 AM (instead of the scheduled start time of 9:00), we're getting out just as they're coming in. The whole morning crew appreciates that—here's hoping my comments had some small influence. The supe may not be too pleased, as clean up now starts at 7:15 PM, an hour and a quarter later, which likely means he'll be staying later. T.S.—we're the ones paying for and putting up with the 'service' and the 'supervision', he's the one getting paid. It's our turn for a little consideration. The rest of the day was largely disappointing. Sam, from the front office, randomly dropped in to the course room to check the checklists of a couple of the sauna students, self included, and set "targets" for the course session this day; didn't meet mine, didn't go back later to make it up either, despite his encouraging me to go to night class (until 9:45 PM). Pass. I done my time, and spending even more of the day and most of the night there isn't going to get me home any quicker, and a paper certificate that I can't even put on my résumé, for digesting boiled-down recovery philosophy, doesn't quite qualify as extra credit worth working towards.

One of the sexy counselor trainees sat outside next to me at dinner, apparently unable to find anywhere else, and I tried to strike up a conversation, she was responsive but not engaging, and left without so much as a "so long". No mail. No reception. But at least an hour of privacy and peace, with classical music on KUSC, then some reading until lights out.

Thursday, September 13, 2012

A fairly good day so far: good sleep, paper ready, decent sauna spell (got to start early because the other supe was working), and then, as I'd fulfilled my class quota for the week, I took the rest of the day off. Spent "third period" going through the *Asian Tribes* book and making some sketches, first in a while, glad to work. A number of people came by and complimented. Got to the chow line in good time, then kicked it for a while—waiting for this evening sauna cleaning, "white glove" tonight, which isn't much more rigorous than any other day.

To Tom fm Margaret

Dear Tom,

I have wondered how you've dealt with going from being a hermit to having to share space with other people constantly. I imagine it makes for a shock to your system... And I can't imagine that everyone in the facility is farting sunshine and roses. I would guess that the grumpies is the normal there. Ultimately, it is about what you get out of it. You might not buy the program whole hog, but you might get some self-discovery and learn some ways to avoid killing yourself too young. And, you might come out of this being able to tolerate other people better, which is a skill we all need. And, it sounds like you're feeling the buddings of some motivation to do something outside of yourself. You'll get there.

My job is pretty much what I wanted to do when I was growing up. I'm the "boss" so I have some power. We are a private non-profit, so we have fewer rules and regulations to deal with (unlike if we were say, the Dept. of Social Services), I know when I put my head down at night that my energies went towards making the community safer and to serve people... Not earn profits for fat, rich, balding, old men with Swiss bank accounts. Ninety-five percent of the clients we work with are actually nice people who have lives way out of their control, and/or were in the wrong place at the wrong time with the wrong people. I frequently look at some of the folks I serve and think to myself "one or two decisions made differently, and your life would be wholly different. One or two decisions made differently, and I could be living your life."

I visited Granny over the weekend. That was depressing. She has lived too long. She would be horrified if she knew this is what she'd end up being. I brought her a photo of us taken about thirty years ago. I'm pretty sure she recognized herself, I also brought her some fudge and managed to get her to eat a little. There is no mental stimulation whatsoever there. She did reach out and trace, with her finger, the heart design on the fudge box. I've suggested to family who will see her more often that something she can manipulate with her hands would be helpful. Granddaddy was there too. She kept shooting looks of pure anger at him. I'm pretty sure everyone in the family understands your sentiment of finding Granddaddy a pain in the ass. There was a time, when we would visit, Bruce would stay in my room the whole time, save for meals. Granddaddy just loves to pick arguments with people. One time he went off on this thing about how Roosevelt knew the Japanese were going to bomb Pearl Harbor, but wanted in the war, so did nothing to stop it or protect the people there. That is simply not true. He wouldn't let it go. WWII is Bruce's area of expertise... When Bruce walked out of the house to avoid cursing Granddaddy out, Granny told him to go apologize to Bruce. Instead, as he followed Bruce down the driveway, he kept at it. Again, I think the reason no family member has volunteered to help the grandparents is because no one wants to deal with Granddaddy.

Dad has told me, over the years, that I should write about the *women in our family and call it "Angry Women." I'm starting to think that what I should do is write about the men in our family and call it "The Last Male Chauvinist Pig." Maybe this is another reason you and Chris, both, seem to have broken away from the family... You can't be like the men who were your role models. You, both, have to be your own men... Deciding who you are is tough. I had lots of feminist role models growing up. I got to see other ways of living beyond being a housewife. In some ways, I probably had more choices than you guys did, at least in terms of role models and knowing that I could craft my own rules.*

I'll try to pop some books in the mail soon.

Love you.
Margaret

Monday, September 17, 2012

Well, Sunday was a bit of the usual—five hour sauna program and three rounds of chores, the roommate having a bit of a fit over health issues. The usual high school bullshit around "campus"... but I did manage to do a bit more sketching, and one of the supes asked if I thought I was done with sauna, and if so to write something to that effect for the case supervisor.

And, this morning, after showing up early as usual, the supe today said he "didn't have my folder"; which meant it was under review and I could piss off until somebody came and told me where to go, so, there was an interview with the examiner, then another C.S. review, then the attest, then re-taking the four IQ/ aptitude tests. Don't really know if thirty-one days in the box improved me, but I did sweat gallons and lost a couple pounds, and with the exercise and food and vitamins, I've got to be in better shape than I started, right? And, at the very least it's another month sober, right? Slight hump, I've got to finish the fucking "alternative" course book, "Helping someone overcome addiction" before I can start the next "real" course, Book 3: Learning Improvement. So I banged away at that until almost ten-o-fucking clock, seven-plus hours of course... and it's about time for some more fucking mail, right?

To Dad fm Tom

Hello—hope all continuing well up your way, the house holding together and plans for the trip still on line.

I'm now twenty-five percent finished with the required courses, although by all accounts the upcoming courses do not take quite as long so I am still hoping for a November release. Early November, I'm hoping. The list of things to do upon return to the world continues to grow, so I don't foresee boredom as being a problem.

Been doing a bit of sketching and jotting down some story ideas in the rare free moments, and getting in some reading and Sudoku when I can. Haven't started <u>The Red Tent</u> *yet, but while in the box did read a Patricia Cornwell novel (*<u>Trace</u>*) and a James Patterson (*<u>See how they Run</u>*), both of which were pretty disposable best sellers that I can't highly recommend. Scrounged a book from the "lounge,"* <u>The Fear</u> *by Peter Godwin, a non-fiction account about Robert Mugabe's reign of tyranny in Zimbabwe—pretty horrific. Makes everything here in the States seem blissfully reasonable by comparison.*

Yes, please activate and forward one of the cards. The card will no doubt be placed in safekeeping, but should be added to the wallet once I get out (and can be used if I'm able to take escorted off campus visits to the movies or elsewhere once the program is half over... I believe...). Also, if any of those balance transfer checks have been forwarded by Joe, please send those as well so that I might fund the student account for weekly extras and necessities.

That about covers it for now—love to Linda and Rhys, and

Love,
Tom

tom crites

To Tom fm Dad

Hi Ya Tom,

All well here. Linda and I drove to eastern Oregon/Washington this weekend where I swam with a group across the Columbia river, not Alcatraz, but fun nevertheless.

Can't say if I've gotten all your letters or not, you tend not to date them so no good reference point. I did get the letter questioning if I got it, but didn't get any letter with instructions about your ATM cards. (I have included them in the box, one [5151] has been activated, the other one has not). Remember that just because you are paranoid doesn't mean they are not out to get you.

I sent them copies of your medical insurance forms, and notified the insurance company first thing when you went in. They are supposed to file a claim from there. There is supposed to be some coverage, but it all takes time.

A couple more books: <u>The Sparrow</u> is one of my favorites—not the quality of Atwood, but some themes I found interesting. I couldn't finish <u>The Gingerman</u>. It's one of the sixties "bad boy" books rebelling against the suit, oh so clever. I just found him a vicious cad and although I don't need to love the main character, I couldn't stomach this one. And I couldn't re-read <u>The Moon is a Harsh Mistress</u>. Enjoyed it long ago, but have read too much really good stuff in the meantime. And his choppy style in this book, "moon-speak" I suppose, put me off a bit.

Take Care.

Love,
Dad

To Margaret fm Tom

Dear Margaret,

Hello! Hope all well in your part of the world and you're enjoying the change of seasons (and the ER hasn't been too busy). It's been another twelve-hour day here, four course periods, plus night course, plus chore (re: the "in charge" position, that's still holding for that area—made the mistake of distinguishing myself by being on time, showing good work ethic and attention to detail, and was rewarded with the thankless task of trying to make others do the same—but, at least it's not cleaning the course bathrooms), and I am beat. But I've still got forty-five minutes to "lights out", a cup of sleepy time tea, and some movie with Gary Sinese and Viggo Mortenson on TV (Albino Alligator), so no complaints! If I hadn't already brushed my teeth I'd be noshing some of the Popcorn Factory's chocolate popcorn, which as weird as it sounds is actually damn good. Thanks again for that!

Finished the sauna program, sweated gallons, got in some exercise each day, mega-dosed on vitamins—didn't experience any of the flashbacks though, despite all of the acid I ate in my day, and the mood swings I did experience pretty much maxed out at irritation at being shut into a small area with twelve half-naked sweaty dudes and listening to competing locker room conversations and bad white boy reggae... so, that was enough of that.

A.M. now laundry, exercise, and studying for a "spot check" on the learning improvement course. Thrill-a-minute here I tells ya.

"Kind of" looking forward to Halloween, for no specific reason except, well, it's Halloween. Maybe the owls and the fog will contribute, but I don't know how or if they "do" Halloween around here. And I left my leatherface mask hanging at home...

That's about the size of it for now, cheers to Bruce. Don't know what to say regarding the grandparents (although Dad did say that grandmother is fighting the staff—good for her! If she's going to go, I'm glad she's going fighting) but, as they say, it is what it is. Feeble, I know, but philosophy can only do so much (and not very much at that).

And with that,

tom crites

Tuesday, September 18, 2012

Finished the addiction book and attested to that, began working my way through "Learning improvement" (Book 3). Actually <u>enjoyed</u> it, looking up the fucking words and everything, acing the "check-ups" and memorization (mostly). Would have gone to night course, but there were only two of us scheduled so that got canceled. All day with the roommate's complaints—physical problems from sauna supplement regimen, heater temp and schedule, staff, etc. Anyway, it's nice to be out of the box and back on a regular schedule, not starting course until 10:00, only having one chore most days, getting a full hour for lunch. Still IC of the evening dining/serving/entry area, and we got cut down to three people on that, but we've got it down.

Friday, September 21, 2012

<u>Two months sober</u>

An interesting day, up fairly early, did laundry and rode the stationary bike yesterday, so skipped all that today. Banged through the early courses, and had the pleasure of a package waiting for me at break: a package from Dad containing books, letter, information, and the latest *Brain Cell* from Ryosuke Cohen in Japan with, yes!, the Planarian Liberation Army logo, again handsomely made into a stamp (ink). On the way out of the room, after putting all that away, I was taking a quick piss before course, and, yes, the toilet tank chose to once again pop the hose that feeds from the cistern (?) into the bowl and spray water out from under the lid, swamping the floor. So, had less than five minutes to mop that up (can't just leave it like that...) and hustle off to class. Finished the last stages of Book 3, final test essay and all, and now have the test first thing in the morning. Due to the perfect schedule I was once again forced to skip dinner, entirely this time as compared to the quick salad of last night and the apple of the night before, in order to start getting ready for the evening chore. I was putting my butt out in preparation for moving a five-gallon up to dining when Lisa called me into her office. She'd received a call from my Dad, and Grandmother died last night. With the Alzheimer's and the weakness of age (ninety), the pain from falls and everything else, it was understood by all that she was done, and ready to die—at least she did pass away in her sleep. Lisa said that (upon my inquiry) although they preferred people not leave the program, in cases of family emergencies things might be worked out if I had to go back east and help take care of things. It's a shame to see the rare, truly good people go—she was one of the smartest, wisest, most talented people I knew. Goodbye, Grandmother, I love you.

So then, on to clean, started banging away; the new girl, second day on the task, disappeared halfway through, the other new guy "left the building yesterday". (Henry, an older cat, he'd had enough of the Oakview experience by the time he completed sauna. It took literally days for them to get him a straight answer and let him out the door. The same thing happened when Maureen, another "older" student who wanted to go—days of no straight answer. Then, word is, they wouldn't let her call a cab from O.R. for a pick-up at O.R.—they dropped her off at a K-Mart to call a cab from a pay phone...) And I finished it all off (a little slap-dash) and I barely got to the empty water bottles back to the rack, washed up and pissed before the graduation fest started. Received my certificate for the sauna program, and my acceptance speech went like this: "you know, some people might say spending thirty-one days in a small box with a bunch of other sweaty half-naked guys is too much, I'm one of those people. And I'm glad I did it anyhow. I feel good, I was (actually) excited to get out of sauna and start Book Three, Learning Improvement, and I'm actually enjoying it, which is unusual because I do not like to study. So thanks to..., etc." As soon as the other certs were out and the actual graduation speeches given, I nabbed a leftover steak and enjoyed it, even cold and w/o horseradish.

To Tom fm Margret

Dear Tom

I wrote that last note and stuck it on my fridge last week, waiting for a day when I could go through my bookshelves and find some books I thought you'd like. It's now a little out of date. Cathy called me this morning, while I was on my way to work, to tell me that Granny died overnight.

Remember when we were kids and we would visit Granny... She always had a candy jar... And we'd attack it like children who'd never seen candy. One of the ways she made sure people felt at home when visiting her was to make sure she made their favorite desserts. For Dad, it was chocolate crinkle cookies and for me it was lemon meringue pie.

Did you know that Granny decided when she was five that she was going to hell? She'd swiped a cookie and her mother wanted her to own up to it. She sent Granny outside to think about it, when one of her brothers came along, he told her that "you'll go to hell if you tell mother a lie". Granny said she balled up her fists and said to herself "fine, I'll just go to hell." When she was in the third grade, she got sent home from school for refusing to sign the temperance pledge. She was the only child in the whole school who wouldn't sign. She said "I'm eight, I don't know what I'm going to do when I'm grown." Irony is, she's never taken a drink. Her father had a severe sensitivity to alcohol and she had a brother who died a morphine addict, so she felt it wouldn't be good to try it, lest she like it too much.

Granny never minced words with me. She was always blunt and honest. As a teenager, I'm sure I was a terror. But, she didn't back down, and she was just as stubborn as I was. She made sure I knew I was loved, unconditionally. I know I pretty much lost her a few years ago, when she first started slipping. But, there were those glimpses of who she used to be. I hate that her life ended the way it did. She wouldn't have wanted to live that long.

m

To Margaret fm Tom

Hello, and good morning (although it's probably closer to midday in your region). Hope all as well as possible out your way—I received the word about Grandmother's passing and spoke to Dad briefly. Although I was truly sad to hear that she's gone, by all accounts she was still present enough to know she didn't want to live that way, and went out finally as peacefully as possible. I was thinking that I should have gone to see her sometime before, but, I also think it better that my last physical memory of her was when I was able to go out a couple years back and she was still alert, and able to take me on one of her amazing mountain walks.

I will always remember her as one of the smartest and wisest, not to mention most talented, people I have known. And she was also instrumental in encouraging and teaching me how to draw, more so than any formal instructor I've known, so I will continue to value that for the rest of my life. I've been keeping an eye on a fungal growth on a tree stump here I have dubbed "the blob", something that started out looking like a thin trail of yellow sap and has grown every day until it now resembles a multihued, multilayered little alien city— looking at it this morning I couldn't help but think "Granny would have loved to paint that..."

Dad said that, per her wishes, there would be no ceremony or service, the scattering had already been scheduled and Cathy will be handling the will as executor. But if the family needs help with the house or grounds, moving, cleaning, clearing, etc., please let me know (I've told Dad this as well). I'm not much of a handyman, but do have some manual labor experience that might be of use. I've spoken to the staff here about this, and they've indicated that they "might" be able to work with me on this.

On another note, things continue to move forward here: Passed my test for "Book 3" (out of 8), the "Learning improvement course", and aced it (100 percent), so it actually did me some good right away—I hate studying and being tested, but didn't mind this so much. So, that much is good. On to the next steps, which will make me "upstat", eligible for brief trips off campus. Maybe I'll get to see a movie for the first time in two months! Other than that, all just shoving along.

That's about the size of it for now, just wanted to drop a line of condolence and consideration and memorial.

Hope you're doing alright,

Love,
Tom

To Tom fm Dad

Hello Tom,

We were all saddened by my mother's death, but I'm sure she was relieved. The saddest part was seeing her pain and confusion the few weeks before when I was there before she went into the care facility. There was no ceremony/gathering. My brother John is to accompany my father to scatter her ashes in the family cemetery at Benton, Missouri. Not sure what is to become of my father. Remains to be seen if he can care for himself though he remains steadfast in his refusal to accept any help of any kind.

Sent your ATM cards in a box with a couple books. Glad to

hear you continue to move through the program. You mentioned the diarrhea problem—is that a common reaction? Watch out for dehydration—though I know you have always drunk a lot of water.

Glad to hear you are drawing and writing again! Your stay there should give you a lot of material to work with.

We leave on Tuesday 9/25 and return Sunday Oct. 7. I'll try to send any last mail before we take off.

Love,
Dad

P.S. The house loan has been approved so recovering a bit financially. Here is a check to Oakview for the "student account".

To Dad fm Tom

Good morning—hope all as well as possible up your way. From our phone conversation it sounds as if that is the case. You may not actually receive this letter for weeks being in Berlin (you may have chosen an inopportune time to stop drinking however, as I understand Oktoberfest started this last weekend—but even if you don't sample a "mass" or two, it should still be a unique cultural experience), but I wanted to say, again, that I was sad to hear about Grandmother's passing. But, again, by all accounts she was still together enough to know that she did not want to live that way (as no intelligent person would). I can't help but think now I should have gone out to see her one last time, but at the same time I also think that I much prefer to remember her as I was privileged enough to some years ago when she was still sharp and able enough to take me on her amazing mountain walks. I will always remember her as one of the smartest and wisest, strongest and most talented people I have ever known, and I will for the rest of my life remember how instrumental she was in encouraging and teaching me to draw. So much more so than any formal instructor, and I will always cherish that.

On a more positive note, things progressing fairly here—passed my Book 3 ("Learning Improvements") course with 100 percent, so apparently actually managed to learn something in a single week. (I don't like to study, and truly hate being tested—was up front with the staff here from the start that the resentment of this process bordered on a learning disability, but I may be in the process of overcoming that, which is a good thing.) On to the next stage, which should soon make me "upstat" eligible for brief day trips offsite—may be able to catch a movie for the first time in months. Dredd 3D and Lawless are sounding pretty good. Been trying to squeeze in a little sketching, get back into the practice. Joe sent an interesting book, Asian Tribes, which has some great models and designs ideas (some enclosed).

My thanks again for the books, and the cards. Hope the trip is a fine one. And again, please let me know if there is anything I can do regarding the grandparents' estate. I may not be much of a handyman/fit-it guy, but I do have some manual labor experience.

Love,
Tom

Wednesday, September 26, 2012

So. It's been a few days. A few interesting ones. Saturday I took the Book 3 test—it took two-and-a-half hours and four full sheets of legal-size paper to get 100 percent. That's all right. Then started "The Checkouts Book"; about and how to administer the brief section quizzes. Sunday got to do the first white glove campus cleaning, scoring a spot on the pool patio crew, washing windows and tables, scrubbing stones. Had done the white glove of the room earlier (I had the front area this week) and got to do the dining chore again as well. Did a little, very little, bit of sketching, and there was a card game that was supposed to happen, but didn't. Couldn't even catch a decent nap, what with staff fucking coming around to check up/body count every two to ten minutes...

So, Monday. I think I finished the Checkouts Book and started the "Communication and Perception" orientation book. Got my certificate for last week's completion of the "Helping Someone overcome addiction" book at the evening muster, and got to listen to the new estates guy, Derek, tell us that he would be giving lots of "chits" (demerits) because he was, as he said, "kind of an asshole about that". I don't know what the fuck else happened.

Tuesday started off on a shit note as I awakened just after 4:00 in the morning by the roommate fucking around with the windows, bouncing his fat ass around in the bed, moving around in the room and finally banging the door shut on his way out. After half hour or so I crawled out of bed and went up to the main building for coffee –So the rest of that day was great, I had to skip dinner, which looked none too great anyhow, pasta and clams, and had an apple and a cigarette and started the chore early—and still got to class during roll call, earning a chit "where do I contest that?" I asked, and I think I got it lifted after a bit of justification, but then decided to stay for night course when the fucking clay demo I was working on took one-and-a-half hours of "fourth period". And then the night supe, the un-funny Pee-Wee Herman, had me working on it for at least another thirty minutes. So by 9:45 I was pretty sick of the day, hit the sack and actually got eight hours of sleep.

So then, this morning, smooth enough until the word at roll call, when the word was that, according to big IC, "we don't have to tell you when you get chits." Which is kind of a shitty way to do business—if you don't know you've been given a demerit for lateness or some error in the chore, not only would we not be able to work it/them off to be able to go "upstat" (offsite) and avoid Sunday shitwork, but if we don't know there's been a mistake, how are we to know not to make the same one again, right away? Wrote and sent a letter to Joe early when I was in a good mode, got a package of books from Margaret (Stieg Larssen, Patricia Cornwell, Jeffrey Deaver, Michael Crichton), and got a pink sheet in course, which in this case was for keeping my head down and busting my ass. I'm upstat now, by the way, as long as I don't have any chits I don't know about, and as Dad sent a letter and a check for $100 that I received this Monday, I <u>may</u> get off campus this Sunday. We'll see... Fuck I'm tired.

To Tom fm Margaret

Hi Tom:

I like your art work. Some of your designs would make interesting metal work/jewelry. Have you ever done metal work? My co-worker does some wire work jewelry, but it's more beading stuff than creating original works.

When I visited Granny earlier this month, she seemed to recognize that she needed to be polite to me (didn't seem to know who I was, but the years of being female kicked in) but she shot Granddaddy several really viciously angry looks. I mentioned it to Lee, and he said that he sometimes has to remind himself how angry she always was. This kinda surprised me, because I don't think of Granny as being an angry person. I asked Dad about it, and he said that he remembered that there were times she'd get angry, break things, and then go to her sister's for a few days. I told him that I did remember some fairly scary fits (including breaking things) but that I always felt like her outbursts were justified (Granddaddy being a jerk) and never really thought of them as indicative of her personality. I should note, Granny NEVER threw anything at me or hit me. I took the day off to cry my heart out, the day Granny died.

So, you're making progress in the program, but do you see a more positive outlook for yourself? It sounds like you might leave the program physically healthier... But, what else?

Do you know when you'll be discharged in NOV? Do you have a specific plan for when you are discharged?

I am thinking about visiting Dad in Portland during the week before Thanksgiving (much cheaper airfare then)... If you were going to be there, that might seal the deal... But don't feel like you have to manipulate your plans. I can figure out other times to visit Portland in such a way as to run into you.

So, how are the supplies of popcorn holding up? Need more? Flavor requests?

M

Friday, September 28, 2012

Not a bad day—worked on the clay models and the "Practical Assignments" for Building Affinity in course, and worked my way back into the TRs portion of Book 4. I'd received a massive care package from Margaret yesterday, candied popcorn (from Moose Munch—"Delirious Snacks"), <u>ten bags</u> in multiple flavors—in a word, gooder'n hell; used one to pay the debt of that pack of Virginia Slims 120s that had been let go but I didn't want hanging over my head, and used the offer of one for a pack of Marlboro Reds, which was freely given instead (!). Got through the chore (yesterday two people dropped out of the four person crew—if it hadn't been for a great young lady who just happened to be passing through when I was explaining this to the IC, and offered to help, we'd have been sunk—as it was we got to course late, but didn't get chitted.), and I even got my "upstat" request approved to go offsite on Sunday—hopefully to see *Looper* (but almost anywhere would be good). As long as the returning staffer they call "Chitler" doesn't live up to his promises too proudly. The graduation "ceremony" was short and sweet, got my Book 3 cert, and gave a speech: "I liked this course book. It actually teaches you how to study, which I surely needed. Not only that, but it teaches you study skills that you can actually use to help you get through the course. And nobody appreciates that more than a resentful slow-learning bastard like myself. On top of that you learn a bit of language trivia—like the fact that the word "stimulate" comes from the Latin root "stimulare", which literally means "to prick with a stick". So I'd like to thank Richard, our course supervisor, for pricking me with that stick and getting me through the course. Thank you, cheers."

I didn't have time to sit down and enjoy dinner, but there were still steaks left over so I nabbed one of those, enjoyed it even without horseradish (there's always salt!), had a glass of milk, a cigarette, and some moose-a-liciousness. Kicking back now, one of the *Amityville* pictures on the "This" channel. Tazo "calm" tea—

Sunday, September 30, 2012

A full day, and by and large, a good one. A good hot one—it had to be eighty-plus up here on the hill. Got up early, did the coffee and cigarette, but noticed right way that there was no water pressure in the room. And none in the main building either—tried to start a new pot of coffee, and "refilling" the machine says. Talked to night desk, they got on it, but got no immediate response. Not a problem... Did some Sudoku (flunked two, got one finally—all medium), enjoyed the full moon, looked out for the paper. People started trickling in to the dining room. Gripes and groans and chit and chat.

Water came back on, breakfast was served. And Cindy from the front desk was kind enough to bring me my paper when it arrived. I thanked her kindly, and immediately had to put my hand on it when the ex-con/hustler who just returned to campus reached for it (after my deliberately leaving it banded and bagged after telling Cindy I'd read it later, as by now there were six or so vultures looming about, having gone through the tattered remnants of the papers from a couple days past: as I've seen before, the second a new paper hits the deck it literally gets torn to pieces—one section here, another there, sports gone [fine], business gone [fine], sections ending up inside, outside, sauna, bathroom...). We gave each other a funny look, he laid off and I went back to breakfast, he reached for it again, and I put my fist on it again. "Aw come on you freak," he said half-jokingly. "I wasn't gonna open it, I..." I looked at him, "you spend two weeks and $94 organizing a subscription, you can do whatever you want with it." That pretty much settled that. Although he did ask if it really took two weeks and I started to tell him exactly why that was, and he got the picture and laid off again.

Breakfast eaten went back to the room and got an early start on the white glove action—my turn for the bathroom this week. Spent over an hour on that in anticipation of Chitler's visit tomorrow. Brief break, then back up to the main building for campus white glove. Got the patio area again, so spent an hour or so in the sun sweeping, scrubbing, and hosing. Checked the chit list, which I'd been checking all week, and busting my ass to keep clean, and saw that I again had no demerits—was a bit worried that I might have been tagged in the course Saturday morning for wearing my knit cap at roll call (it was fucking <u>cold</u>), even though I pulled it off before actually starting class work (and had ideas of what I might do had that happened), but squeaked by, making me eligible for my first upstat!

Went hunting for update on upstat: nobody seemed to know exactly who would be doing the escorting or arriving with the van. But he showed up shortly and we headed out straightaway. My vote was for the movies, as was the vote of the two others going out; apparently, however, movie schedules are not checked prior to leaving, and no consensus was taken. So we showed up at the theater and there was a bit of uncertainty, an "um..." period. At 3:45 our options were limited: it looked like it might be between *End of Watch* or *Nemo 3D*, neither of which I wanted to see (*Watch* didn't look good, and I did not want to see a kid's movie)... But _Looper_ started at 4:00, and as nobody was dead set, that was my diplomatic suggestion. Which passed the vote, so that's what we did.

After, as nobody was in the mood for a sit-down meal at the neighboring Applebee's we went to the beach instead. Just a few minutes, but the waves and sea air, the eucalyptus and ice plants nearby, and the shells (picked up a couple, gotta do that), all made for a beautiful (short) time. A quick stop at Taco Bell, having no allure for me when sober, it was still a change. And it still surprises me how many Mexicans eat at the Taco Bell, here in CA where there are loads of Hispanic and Mex restaurants. Not in Watsonville, I guess. Got back to campus, and I found that there was still Asian food (sushi rolls, chicken skewers, egg rolls) leftover from dinner. Enjoyed some of that, finished Godwin's _The Fear_ and got to sleep early, for what would be eight-plus hours despite the changing temperature (hot to cold). A good day, I have to say (oh yeah, picked up a few copies of the local Santa Cruz free weeklies at the theater as well!).

Prehab 2010

Spring, 2010

Many many changes: alcoholism increased to all day drinking, barely ate anything (some days nothing at all). But was in remarkably good humor most of the time. Got along exceptionally well with the neighbors, friends, strangers, etc. But physical and mental condition definitely weakening. On St. Paddy's Day 3/17/10, I had been unable to sleep until 3 or 4 AM the previous night; woke up around 10:30 AM, went out after 11:00 to take out the mail, then went around the corner to Red Carpet Liquor and bought a couple bottles of Boone's Farm (which turns out to be a flavored beer, not a wine as I'd always thought. A good morning drink; like a tall bottle of soda pop with a 4% alcohol content), a couple bottles of cheap white wine, and a tall bottle of Bushmill's Irish whiskey. There was no solid Paddy's Day plan except that Joe was making a brisket and we were going to drink our asses off.

I laid the bottles out on the table, and decided that before I cracked any of them I would do one responsible thing that day and check the mail to see if I had bills to pay. I went downstairs, and the next thing I remember was a pair of paramedics sliding me onto a gurney and loading me into an ambulance. Apparently, as told to me by some of the neighbors later, I just passed out and cracked my skull on the concrete courtyard. The wife of the landlord saw this (fortunately) and called 911; apparently I was bleeding and foaming at the mouth. The next few days were a blur, what with the head injury and the drugs being pumped into me (I had so many injections and IV attachments that my arms were black and blue), but I do have some recall: an out-of-body experience looking down on my body, face-down in blood with a gash on the back of the head; fighting everyone at the hospital, paramedics, orderlies, patients (I'm even told I took a swing at a pregnant nurse); pulling out my own catheter, and only realizing what I was doing halfway through—and going through with it all the way, so much pain and blood, I pissed blood for two days. Had a CAT scan the first night, which showed some bleeding in the brain. The lab was a trip; the ceiling was composed of lighted panels displaying overhanging flowering branches against a blue sky—it reminded me of the suicide room in *Soylent Green*.

I spent a couple days in ICU, a day or two on floor six or seven and then the rest of the time on floor five, rehab. Not too bad really, though I had to learn to walk and use memory and communication again (I'd had a second CAT scan the second night which showed no additional bleeding. So the situation was that I basically had a damaged bursa that would heal, inside my brain.) I'd given Lisa my keys before the ambulance took me away so she could lock my apartment (she and Celia were kind enough to come see me at the emergency room), and gave her Joe S.'s phone number. He would eventually be the one to pick up my mail and haul it to the hospital so I could pay my bills.

3:30 AM: More nonsense this morning as the nurse woke me up for the second time for medication and blood pressure. Couldn't get back to sleep so did leg exercises and read some of Fleming's *Live and Let Die*.

5:30 AM: The staff here are generally incredibly nice and knowledgeable, but some of the nurses are really getting on my tits about using the bathroom. I accept the fact that I have to use the walker, but I'm also supposed to let them know before I go, and again when I'm finished. Sometimes they'll even poke a head in to see if I'm okay. Fucking infant I am. Met Faraja, the new nurse. Did my leg exercises. Finished *The Return of Lono* by O.A. Bushnell, about Captain Cook's last voyage to Hawaii in 1779.

9:00 AM: PT—worked the leg exercises with Juanita, didn't hurt as badly as yesterday, and as usual we had a very entertaining and unusual conversation.

10:45 AM: OT—played Wii with Kristen; a rather difficult

boxing game that required multiple hand and feet movements. Not a bad way to pass a therapy session.

2:15 PM: ST. Yuki came by with a game of Scrabble: we only got part of one game finished, but through sheer dumb luck my first word (bindery) topped her total score.

The stay was much nicer than expected (I still don't know how much I'm going to have to pay after insurance): the food, although cafeteria-style, was plentiful, varied and tasty for the most part, I had my own room with a view of downtown, limited cable, and some of the interns and therapists were both nice and incredibly hot. Had to use a wheelchair for a while and a walker most of the rest of the time, and some of the Filipino attendants were pretty annoying, but all in all my health improved radically from the condition I was in when I went in. I weighted 134 lbs going in and 150.5 lbs going out.

While on floor six or seven, in a room nearby, an old man was dying, literally dying. He was wailing and crying out, although I couldn't tell whether this was from pain, fear, or the sheer knowledge that death was approaching. The man's adult son was there, telling his father to be strong and everything would be all right. The son's two daughters were there as well, but I don't think I heard a wife or mother. Eventually, with a final sound that I just don't know how to describe, the old man died. His son started weeping, having just seen his father pass away in front of him. And his daughters started singing and dancing around the room—they were happy that grandpa was dead, because now they wouldn't have to go to the hospital anymore.

Today was my last day at the hospital. Most of my things were already collected, so kicked back and enjoyed a breakfast of French toast, sausage, orange juice, hot cocoa and milk. Read some of Mailer's *The Naked and the Dead*, said some good-byes, set up some follow-up therapy, and at around 11:00 AM, Joe S. came by to pick me up. Got home and found that not only had he and Bonnie cleaned the entire house—some of which hadn't been touched in a year of alcoholism. Kitchen and bathroom spotless, laundry done and folded (and there was a mountain of that shit just sitting there when I went down), even disorderly stacks of tapes, CDs, games and DVDs organized into custom-made boxes and stacked out of the way. Amazing. I'd been told they had done some cleaning, and on top of the bill delivery, I'd already promised them dinner, but I also sent Joe away with a Japanese bondage drawing he and Bonnie had been favoring, along with a couple DVDs I knew he'd hate and O.A. Bushnell's *The Return of Lono.*

It was good to be home, alone. The hospital had wanted me to have someone in the apartment 24/7 for a week, "just in case", and somehow the hospital thought my father would be doing this. (He had come down for Easter, which was not a fun time; tried to be polite and social, but despite some burst of conversation, we mostly looked at the walls or each other; at one point it got to be so dull and awkward that he started reading a cycling magazine he'd brought and I took a nap.) And I told him in no uncertain terms that this would not be happening. Three weeks in a hospital, and then a week more in a one-bedroom apartment with someone I didn't want to see in the first place? Sure I'm ungrateful, and a dick, but being a resentful cunt that I am, I will never forgive the arrogant bully he was during childhood, the cowardly abusive bastard who put his precious career above everything else and treated me like shit for the first twenty years of my life. So, no to that. Arranged for Johnny and Lisa that we'd get in touch a few times every day instead to make sure I hadn't fallen and couldn't get up. Of course I can't drink anymore; I don't mind if it kills me, but if I have another cerebral incident that turns me into a retard, that would be the worst. Laying off the pot as well, that is until I'm sure my memory, balance, and thought processes are all back to as close to 100 percent as possible, but will probably have to just lay off of everything.

Spent most of the early part of the day on small chores.

Johnny brought by an excellent Portobello, cheese and hot sauce quesadilla, and around 3:00 a bunch of us got together for a barbeque to sort of celebrate my return home, which I thought was a pretty nice gesture. Celia and her brother Eli were there, as was our mutual friend Bill. We BBQed at Joe A.'s and ate at Johnny and Lisa's: burgers, hot links, 'tater salad, coleslaw, watermelon. Good stuff. Everyone else was drinking and smoking, but I had to limit myself to Vernor's ginger soda. I'm going to have to find a beverage I can slug down like I used to do the booze; if I just switch to soda I'm going to turn into a rotten-toothed diabetic. A good time was had and everybody pretty much called it an early night.

Got up early and went to Kinko's to copy some medical and tax shit, came home and started writing a review of *Eagles over London*. Called the insurance company re: the $1,300 ambulance bill I received, and not only does it look like they've got that covered but the majority of my hospital bill should be covered as well. That sounds a little too good to be true, but we'll see once the statements start rolling in. Did some spot vacuuming and cleaning. Did some pork rind reviews. Getting pissed about the tax situation: they didn't send out forms and instructions this year, and the Post Office doesn't seem to stock them. Johnny picked me up the State forms and downloaded the Feds, but without the instruction book I can't complete the 1040EZ and without the 1040 I can't complete the State. Tried looking at the IRS.gov site online, and only got more frustrated. Tried opening the Adobe file for forms (and hopefully instructions): "file is corrupted and cannot be prepared". Pissed. Started watching *The Invention of Lying*, which was fucking great; got tired, hit the sack.

Was supposed to get picked up by the St. Mary Medical Center transport van at 9:00 AM this morning for insurance review and physical therapy evaluation. But even after calling me three or four times for directions the guy didn't show up until 9:45, I barely made it to my 10:00 appointment (I was supposed to be in at 9:30 for processing), but the lovely May didn't mind and she put me through my paces with a smile. And she didn't seem to think I really needed much PT: I scored fifty-five out of fifty-six on her series of strength and balance tests. I have a speech therapy evaluation with the lovely Yuki (who I know from rehabilitation) tomorrow, so we'll try to figure out how to balance the twenty PT/ST sessions insurance covers per year. When I tried to leave I found out the van driver wouldn't be available for twenty minutes, and practically had a room full of people also waiting for rides. Fuck it, I though, it's only about ten blocks, I'll walk it. I bet I got home before the fucker even got back to the hospital. After a bit of a rest I set out again, determined to find some goddamn IRS information. Hit my Post Office, which only had the State forms, but picked up some stamps and got a copy of the comix zine *Brain Food* in my PO Box. Headed over to the public library and, hallelujah, the kind old lady behind the counter directed me to a mountain of forms and instruction books. Hit the "Friends of the Library" book sale and picked up *Back to Bologna* by Michael Dibdin, *Nature Girl* by Carl Hiaasen, *The Mayan Glyph* by Larry Baxter, *The Ruins* by Scott Smith, and *The Bourne Identity* and *The Bourne Supremacy* by Robert Ludlum—all for $5.25! Home again, fun with taxes and letters to prepare. Whups, turns out because I didn't earn any money at all in 2009 (other than interest), I don't have to file at all. Damn...

Had my speech therapy evaluation this morning; had an early appointment (9:00 AM) and the vans weren't running yet, so I hoofed the eleven blocks and still got there early. Worked with Yuki, the super-cute therapist I'd worked with on the fifth floor; did okay on most tests, but not 100 percent on everything. We agreed with May that ST was probably more important than PT, so next week will have two ST sessions and one PT. Came home to do some reviewing, typing and internet research. Joe dropped by later to invite me over to a dinner party, Johnny and Lisa and Celia were already there and Joe had whipped up a huge meal of salad, garlic bread, and spaghetti with turkey meatballs. Very nice. Much laughter and joking, I passed on the wine and weed and instead opted for an aloe Vera king drink, mango flavor, that I picked up at the 99¢ store—pretty damn good. Watched Herzog's remake of *Bad Lieutenant (Port of Call, New Orleans)*, which sucked ass compared to Ferrara's original. Strange, without alcohol it just seems like there's so much to do; busy with one thing or another all day, passing out naturally at 10:00 PM.

Had my follow up appointment with Dr. Ali this morning; he was the one who initially treated me in the ER after my head injury from the fall on 3/17/10. I'd kind of been dreading this, as I had been really rather out of control at that time, and I was a week late with my appointment. (Should have been between 4/16-4/23, but the metro online trip planner had been giving me errors and my street map gave the grid block for his street as being far east from his actual street address—out past the Long Beach airport. But Yuki helped me out with this the other week in speech therapy) anyway, took the 61 bus up Atlantic, filled out the forms (didn't get a copy of the arbitration agreement though...). Had the standard tests and measurements done (weight: 147, with shoes, clothes and keys, blood pressure: 105/70, pulse: 70, height: 6'1"), and after some waiting saw the doc, who couldn't have been nicer. Complemented my appearance, after a brief chat said I seemed very cohesive and functional, and other than saying a twelve-step program might be a good idea, said there really wasn't much else to do but come back in another year.

We both agreed that I was lucky to have apparently recovered, and so quickly, from a severe head injury. Picked up a foot-long veggie patty sammich at Subway on the way home, then sat and read Carl Hiaasen's *Nature girl* with tranny porn in the background. (Finished Norman Mailer's *The Naked and the Dead* yesterday, and read all of Harry Harrison's *Make Room! Make Room!*). Got a letter from Dad in the mail, just chatty, no judgment or attitude, so gave him a call, and after a brief talk to Linda gave him the health status update and talked a bit, soothing out my abrupt rudeness of our last conversation while I was still in the hospital. Said he might send me a banjo...?

Finally went to the grocery store, stocking up canned soup/chili, snacks, salad, bananas. Also bought: <u>RUM</u>. Plans for the day: do laundry (some unthinking twat left the washer full of underwear yesterday), sweep the patio and bleach-washed the deck chairs to make for a little reading/ drinking space, hit the 99¢ store for juice and wafers, and by Red Carpet Liquor to buy: <u>BEER</u>. It's been seven weeks since the accident, seven weeks since I've had a drink, and I don't feel any smarter or happier. Feel as out of place with people as always, and am still prone to spells of depression and hopelessness. So, again with the drinking. Just not the all-day-long-starting-with-Boone's-Farm-bubbling-down-the-throat-before-even-sitting-down-then-moving-on-to-a-bottle-of-wine-drunk-straight-from-the-bottle-and-starting-to-sip-on-the-bottom-shelf-vodka-before-the-wine-is-empty. Although if I can't get a job and end up having to pay the entire hospital bill, well, that's me finished. Anyway...

To Tom fm Margaret

Dear Tom:

I'm glad to hear from you. I suppose you're doing some form of physical therapy? How is that going? Did the recent S. Cali earthquake affect you folks? I never can really get straight in my brain how close or far towns are from the major cities.

You said in your letter that you are fairly angry with Dad for not being more active in stopping/preventing Fran's abuses. I think you are right. And, in fact, it's fairly normal in cases where kids are abused, that they have more anger towards the "non-offending" parent. It's easier to write off the offending parent as "messed up" or "bad"... it is harder to reconcile the reactions of the other parent... The other adult in the house, the one who had power or should have known better. And, for a really long time, I had the same resentments towards Dad. I can tell you that he has told me that he still feels guilt over his lack of action back then. He did admit to me at one time that he was so miserable with Fran, that he volunteered for every trip that would take him away from home. It wasn't until much later, when things fell apart, that he realized that in doing that he'd sacrificed us to Fran. I think he kinda hoped that we were young enough we didn't really understand what was happening. It isn't an excuse, but possibly an explanation.

I also think it isn't fair/right of you to compare what you experienced with what I experienced. Even when I was a kid, when Fran was terrible, I would ball up my fists and say to myself "you're not my real mother." And, in a way, I think that was what protected me from serious, lasting damage. But, even as a kid, I knew that you and Chris didn't have that luxury.

I have heard stories that Fran did physically abuse you before I was adopted. Dad once told me that he had to physically stop Fran from going into your nursery because he "knew" she was going to kill you for crying. Of course, I just made the guilt even worse when I heard this by saying "and you had more children with this woman?" I don't really regret compounding the guilt... I don't think he should have had more children with Fran... And I think he should have scooped you up and left Fran then. Dad has also told me that he tried to find a way to divorce Fran and keep us kids. He (and Granny) told me that he went to lawyers in California and Colorado... And they all told him that he would get me because there was documented evidence of abuse... But that given that you and Chris were her biological children and the abuse was more emotional/psychological, no judge would take you away from Fran. Dad also told me that Fran would tell him that if he ever left her, he would never see you and Chris alive again... And he knew she wasn't talking about moving to New Zealand. He has also told me that he regretted not sending you and Chris to Granny too.

As for you thinking of yourself as a "bad brother"... I have NEVER thought that. Granny has said that one of the things she found most unforgivable about Fran was what she did to our relationship. Granny says that when I was adopted, you were absolutely thrilled to be a big brother... That you doted on me... That you and I were very close. And Fran got jealous of the relationship and actively destroyed it. I've heard that she once slapped a complete stranger in a store because he told her I was cute... But didn't gush over you too. (I think fast talking kept her from being charged.) I also remember that any time Dad tried to "stick up" for me... She would scream that he loved "that bastard" more than his own children. (If you recall, my bedroom in Livermore had a common wall with theirs... I heard most of their arguments.)

Please don't feel that you were a bad brother. You reached out to me when we were teenagers... And I always appreciated our correspondence. You also told me things that helped me feel less abandoned... Like, you once told me that you sometimes found Dad setting an extra place at the table. I needed to hear those things when you told them to me.

I'm pretty sure that Fran was as terrible a parent to you as she could have been. And, I think that Dad was kind of a coward in how he did/didn't deal with it. But you know, somewhere along the line, we ended up all being decent people. (Channeling Stuart Smally a moment... People like us, gosh darn it.) Perhaps it is our own strength of character that made us not grow up to be axe murderers... Or maybe jumbled in there they did something right... But we did grow up to be decent people... If not just a tad flawed in our own little ways. Once I realized that, I didn't care as much about the past. I don't forget it. I don't say it's all swell and dandy... But I think it's less important than what I'm doing now. I also have pretty good boundaries in terms of how much I let Dad in. The stuff with Granny this past year has meant that I needed to have more interaction with him, but for the most part, I think we regard each other with a polite respect but limited affection. I think we all have to find that balance between what allows us the level of contact that serves us without feeling obligated or taxed.

I would like to rekindle our correspondence, if you want to. I do miss having a big brother. Especially since you're cool, and I'm kinda a dork.

Love,
M

Winter, 2010

<u>Sober since 11/21/2010</u>

Not much of a year here: very little art work accomplished. Two alcoholic fugue states ending in head injuries and hospital stays (each requiring having to learn to walk again—just stopped using a cane last week). May have to pay an additional $45K in bills for those; believe my health insurance has a lifetime maximum of $92K, and I've racked up $135K so far this year already ($75K for three weeks at St. Mary's Medical Center in April, $62K for one week at Los Alomitos Medical Center in November—much less nice than St. Mary, and much more expensive. Fuckers—almost as much for one week as three weeks at the other place?). Accommodations not as good (was moved from a two-bed room into a four-bed with three dying guys), food not as good, bed alarmed so I couldn't get up at night by myself (!?).

Been trying to catch up on things since getting out of the hospital; cleaning, filing, drawing, writing, not drinking or getting high, both in an attempt to get my shit straight and to prepare for the intensified job hunt in 2011. Drinking a lot of coffee though, and smoking a lot of cigarettes (brought my first pack in almost four years last month). Eating a lot of candy too, but also eating real meals as well, the lack of which, on top of the lack of real sleep and countless bottles of vodka (my visitors must have been put off by the sea of empties and plastic bags filling the apartment, not to mention the filthy sinks and feet-high piles of dirty laundry). Even stopped answering the phone again, checking email and paying bills. Many thanks to Joe and Bonnie for the cleaning party we had here when I got out of Los Al: place got picked up for the first time in a long time (treated all to dinner at Bai Plu Thai and Sushi restaurant after).

Went up to San Francisco to visit my Dad and his wife Linda. Had recently bought a nice Bailey hat, don't know the exact style (bowler?), but had wanted a semi-formal topper that was weather-resistant, the kind of thing you could wear with a trench coat in bad weather. Also recently had the old man's fifty-year-old alligator coat (vintage wool trench) repaired and cleaned, and thought they went well together as a swank ensemble, rather. With the hat, coat, beard and cane, my father took one look at me and said, "you look like a Hasidic Jew." When I wore the same outfit on the way home, I rode a shuttle bus to Long Beach from LAX, and the second-to-last people off were a German guy and his British girlfriend: as they got off we did the anonymous "Merry Christmas", "Happy Holidays" exchange. And as the bus diver prepared to slide the door shut behind them, German guy leaned in and said, "oh, and Happy Hannukah." Oi!

Rehab *Third Month*

To Margaret fm Tom

Hello! Thank you for your letters, and also for the excellent dual care packages! Books and most excellent candy popcorn ("like crack" another student said upon having a share, which, colloquially, means so good it's addictive)!

Not sure what the immediate plans for release are: I am making progress, but taking the slow steady approach so not sure if I'll be out by Thanksgiving, as was my goal. I do have a growing list of things to do/accomplish once I get back to the world, aside from the immediate details of cleaning house (woefully neglected) and catching up on/ deleting 6,000 emails, there's the job hunt, looking for a new apt. (everybody parties in Long Beach—a new environment might be good...), perhaps in the Highland Park area, which my sober friends in Sierra Madre say is good, reasonable, supportive of the arts, etc., and perhaps get behind the wheel of a car again after, what, twenty- something years?

Aside from the pain in the ass of owning a vehicle (not to mention the expense), I was a definite liability in that regard—I did literally choose to drink rather than drive, not a noble realization, but at least one that didn't lead to harming anyone else, physically, for which I am grateful. And there's the art, the writing, the cooking... boredom is not on the horizon. But there will also be some definite down/home time. Got out on the "upstat" pass yesterday, off campus for the first time in two months, and even seeing the suburbs and strip malls was a perk (the beach, too).

Hope all continues to continue well, and,

Love,
Tom

Friday, October 5, 2012

October. Bit of a heat wave lately, 100°, but back to cold/cool now. Sat a bit during a break, enjoying the sun and cool weather, some breeze, palm trees and cirrus clouds, purty sunset, too. Moon waning now, but a few days ago full and beautiful—you could see the whole rabbit.

Ah, woke up at 4:00 AM this morning to piss, and for some reason could not get back to sleep. Usually able to. Got up again after forty-five minutes and went up to the big house, "Twitch" was there already, already in manic self-conversation mode. Day moved alright, four on dinner chore for the moment, skipped dinner again and still barely had time for a piss and a smoke before graduation. And what a fest that was—one fucker who had a certificate plus a student-of-the-week award hammered it up each time, and in the S.O.W. award (fitting, that), worked in, "it's all about being a good person". This from a guy who talks all manner of trash about people when they're not around, calling guys pussy, prick, retard, talking about wanting to beat them down, and then acts the best buddy when he sees them next. Same with the ladies, only from a more "manly" angle. I had to listen to that shit regularly in the sauna, and now in the room. Always, always, talking shit. "It's about being a good person". And some moody fucker graduating, who may be coming back to stay on staff. And then (and then), looking forward to a left over steak (Friday being steak night) after... not a one. Fuck. I'd had an apple before the chore, so just went back to the room and had tea and some of Margaret's excellent candied popcorn. Still not gelling with anyone here, young crowd still young, very much into themselves, old fuck (self) still old and very much keeping to self. Tired, but not sleepy yet, but not yet 9:00 PM, so will do some paste-up here and get some reading done in a book I picked up in the lounge as I was returning *The Fear*, *The Book Thief* by Markus Zusak—I'm liking it.

Sunday, October 7, 2012

Dream:

Dreamed Sandra was there, somewhere with me. Not <u>with</u> me, but there. At one point we were under the sheets in some bed, and she turned to me and said something about it being good to see me again. I couldn't tell what we were doing there, wherever it was. Or whether she was "with" someone else...

The rest of the dream was surreal as usual, some fancy, some familiar, some not. There was some chore or exercise that I'd blown off and was making excuses for, and there were cats, lots of them—like the ones here.

Monday, October 8, 2012

Day got off to a mixed start; paper here (oh yeah, got a good eight or so hours sleep—top notch), coffee; Twitch making the usual. Gave Charles a lighter to replace the one he gave me weeks ago (on my store order form I asked for a 2-pac of BIC lighters—they skipped it last week, but this week I got a five-pack that came with two free bonus minis). Got a heads up from the roommate, in the period between roll call and first period, re: the previously unannounced pink sheet spot check on the book 4A leading up to TRs—crammed some of that back in, but still ended up having to "clear" a couple words and do some sketches that the supe liked. Got to crack book 4B then, and dive into the next stack of words, demos, and procedures. Found out our chore crew got dicked around again, lost one of the best for one... not so good. Sat through another glad fest of a muster, passed on night course, but managed to bust out a last drill before muster and read up a bit so will start to play the clay tomorrow A.M. Feel alright, I suppose—looking very much forward to sleep. And dreams.

To Tom fm Joe

Tom.

Your letters have been sounding pretty positive lately, so it looks like things may be working... including your brain. Not much to report. Been working in Santa Monica at the estate of a couple of postcard collectors. I know that it doesn't sound like much but imagine what thousands of postcards look like. Besides the normal crap, there were plenty of weird skull, sideshow, disasters, tribal, and other assorted oddball varieties. I picked up the Cthulu compilation paperback for you from amongst the piles of bad sixties and seventies pulp sci fi and horror. Hopefully it's worth reading... if not too bad ya prick. Did pick up some JG Ballard novels, and started reading <u>Crash</u>. Cripes what a book. Bonnie already took it from me when I had her read the first page... so now have to wait until she's done with the damn thing.

Don't worry about missing the chance to hang paper, as the March show still awaits your expert skills. Denis First told me to pass along his regards to you. Went to a buddy's funeral in Cypress last week. Almost everybody there was a total mess due to drugs. Pretty damn glad I moved away from Orange County. We just need to work on moving you next.

Gotta go because Elle's bringing the Philippine contingent along with a Maori tattooist to meet me at the house tonight. Most likely boring time, but you never know. He goes back to New Zealand tomorrow.

Be prepared to start receiving terrible postcards.
I'll get a parcel out to you soon.
Talk to you soon,

Joe

To Tom fm Dad

Hi Tom,

We're back home, after a day's delay when our original flight was canceled and we got to spend a day sitting around the airport before they put us up in a suburban hotel for the night. All well here.

Thanks for the sketches—good to see you drawing again.

While in Amsterdam—great city, canals, thousands of bikes, I did an online search of marijuana growing since I had seen so many pot shops, now nearly every other post on my Facebook page is from some marijuana company. No privacy on the web.

Berlin was okay—the run went well. We left just before Oktoberfest got underway. Many of the group were going on to Munich for the festivities, but we preferred Amsterdam and fewer crowds.

Take care.

Love,
Dad

Wednesday, October 10, 2012

Woke up at 5:30, got coffee and cigarette, hit the stationary bike for a decent sweat (twenty mins) and grabbed a shower. A day of challenges—submitted my "knowledge report" (four pages plus cover) to Ethics early this morning detailing my many reasons for no longer wanting the evening dining IC job and asking that I be replaced. Have to wait and see whether that will be heeded at all, what the option will be if it is, and whether there will be blowback from the "senior head IC" for going over his head. Still have to pass the second part of the objective session training drill, do twenty-three demos, then take a test.

tom crites

To Dad fm Tom

Hello—hope all well up north; it's the rainy season here as I believe it is there.

Things not going so well. Am stuck in a portion of the program called "objective exercises," which are intended to "remedy havingness" (yes, that's a Hubbardism) by improving your abilities to experience things, control your environment, etc., all supposedly leading toward "realizations" that will yield "case gain". I am told that there is no "right" answer for these exercises, that one is to simply follow them and allow the "come to realize moments" to occur, not trying to anticipate any answers or any fake "indicators". This however is not true. Unless you provide the "examiner" with the information they are looking for and your "end phenomena," your collection of "cognitions" and "very good indicators," for each exercise session are not judged to be in proper alignment, you do not pass "go" and you are sent back to repeat the 90-120 minute exercise. Sometimes for days. I am now in the second week of "objectives" and am still on the fifth one; there are fifteen altogether. If I only manage less than five a week it will be perhaps the second week of November before I finish and am allowed to move to the next course, Book 5 (this after having already spent several weeks in and scoring 100 percent on the pre-objectives portion of Book 4); with eight books total, even if I manage to complete one a week (although I of course anticipate difficulties with those as well) it would probably be mid-December before I "graduate". About a month beyond the projected date in November.

My opinions of the institution have not changed from those I held two months ago. I do not agree with their notion of control and reprograming that teaches you not to learn, but to fall in line with their program. I have been learning some things, and would appreciate the chance to learn more, however at this point I am more than doubtful. I am at the point of protesting the course, the fact that there is a "right" answer that they will not provide you, simply "fail" you and make you repeat without explaining why your feedback was "wrong"; for this I will be punished. Any doubts or criticism of the program is interpreted as a "reaction" or a "bad indicator" and the "remedy" for this is to send the student back to a previous course or exercise, to put the student on an "ethics cycle" of interviews and physical labor, or simply put the student in limbo by having their file folder (s) disappear for review. All of these delay forward progress and prolong the duration of the program, as I have seen happen with other students. And which I do not want. If I stop going to course, the same. But I have been playing their game, and I do not appreciate the manipulation and delays. My spot checks, tests, chores, attendance and ethics have all been good or excellent, but not good enough apparently.

My experience here has come full circle now, from near death, depression, and general bad feelings, to a brief period of optimism, hope and inspiration, back down to wondering more than once last week if I wouldn't rather be half-dead on the bathroom floor again.

At this time, after three months of schedules and sobriety, with many ideas and plans in mind, and having weathered the second cold I've had in my time here, I have some hope for the future. Small hope, perhaps, but hope nevertheless. I cannot say how long this will last, and if I am sent into a punishment cycle for questioning the program, there will be a "bad reaction" indeed.

I know that I will be paying for this program for the rest of my life, whether I graduate or not. While I would like to complete the program, if the institution determines to make my time here even more uncomfortable, I may not be willing or able to do so.

Perhaps I'm being alarmist, perhaps my spirits are still low and recovering from the illness and lack of rest of last week, (I could not complain and ask for a day of rest; my "twin" for the exercises, from whom I probably caught the cold, made the mistake of asking for some course periods off, had his folder pulled and was forced to repeat the same exercise over and over because, as he was told by a supervisor, "they just wanted to make sure getting sick wasn't a reaction to that exercise") but if I do complain, consequent reactions may extend to my phone and mail "privileges" being suspended as well, so I just wanted to let you know in advance how things stand.

Thursday, October 11, 2012

11:20 AM: two major hurdles and one minor so far (not counting getting back to sleep mid-morning). Got up at 6:30 AM, managed to get a load of laundry done despite only one somewhat shaky dryer (minor hurdle). Heard at breakfast from head IC that I've been moved to morning course room and bathrooms chore. "Why is that?" I asked, largely about the bathrooms. "I don't know—they just said to move you." OK! Banged that out, no problem. Even with bathrooms, it's still quicker and easier, less stress than that fucking IC gig. And, so far, no blowback. Major, and, after an hour or so and a course of easily answered follow up questions, I got my score—100 percent—Yes! Haven't gone full retard yet. Major. Now I sit comfortably, waiting to be fetched for "objectives orientation". I'm hoping that won't come until after lunch—1:00 PM or later.

To Dad fm Tom

Hello—hope all went well in Berlin, event-wise and culture/ sightseeing—wise. I don't know if they have an Entarte Kunst Museum there or not (a display of types of work the Nazis seized and exhibited as samples of "degenerate art")—a S.F. Chronicle article on such an exhibit currently at Stanford just reminded me of that; in any case it's an interesting period.

Moving along here, managed to ace the Book 4 test as well, still have to do the "objective exercises" which should take two to three weeks (...). But apparently the next four books go much more quickly. So still no definite completion date, but am hoping for some time before the end of November.

Just started <u>The Sparrow</u>, which looks promising. Finished <u>The Fear</u>, by Peter Godwin (Mugabe's reign of tyranny in Zimbabwe, which I may have mentioned before) and <u>The Book Thief</u> by Markus Zusak, which despite the title, I won't bother to steal (little girl in Nazi Germany during the war, etc.)

Just received your letter and package, many thanks! I'd pretty much ignored the film (<u>The Hunger Games</u>) when it came out, as all of a sudden it was such a huge teen thing, but did have the impression the book was supposed to be good/better. I'd seen <u>Promethus</u> when it came out, and was not impressed either. Didn't seem to extend the <u>Alien</u> myth in any good way, or at all, really, and while some of the effects were alright, I much preferred the old pre-CGI action of the original. Finally gained "upstat" status, which meant I got to go with an escorted group to see <u>Looper</u>, which I did like: during the film I kept having the impression that something was missing, but they threw in some elements the reviews didn't mention, and I did find myself thinking of the film for a couple days afterward.

Glad to hear the run went well and you enjoyed Amsterdam—re: all the unsolicited "medicinal" ads/posts on the Facebook page, I think you can set it so only "friends" will be able to post, or at least select a certain post and select the option to hide/ban/remove all posts by that user. Or at least you used to be able to—been so long since I've used it regularly that new "improvements" may have changed that.

Doing some sketching and writing down lots of ideas, so hope to get things back into full swing upon my return. Joe's been suggesting that a move to another area might be a good thing, and I'm thinking he might be right.

Many thanks for the check for the student account –very much appreciated. Hope all continues well and you all weather the changing seasons well in the new abode, but having spent winters in Gaithersburg it shouldn't be too much of a system shock.

Love to Linda and Rhys, and my thanks again.

Love,
Tom

tom crites

To Margaret fm Tom

*Many thanks for the letter and card (love me some monkey action!)—
Just started* The Girl who kicked the Hornet's Nest, *and am enjoying
it very much (thanks for that as well!). Starts off, of course, much
faster than the first; although while I know I read the second one, it
must have been during a period of, ahem, less than crystal attention.*

*Not too much to report of late; aced my recent Book 4 test
(Communication and Perception), and manage to weasel my way
out of the thankless after-dinner IC gig with a four-page report on
exactly why it was so fucked that I had to rush through or skip dinner
to ensure everybody else's mess and slack were picked up. (A little
more diplomatically than that, of course) Boo-hoo, I know, but no
overtime pay or résumé credits, well, prove yourself and move on,
me thinks.*

*Moving on... still have the "objective exercises" to do, which are
supposed to do wonders for me and my "case". And then Books 5-8,
which are supposed to go much faster than the first four. So, still no
definite "day out," but I am hoping for sometime before the end of
November.*

*Love,
Tom*

*Oi! Just got your letter—cheers to the good times in NOLA! Glad you
mentioned absinthe and crawdads, it doesn't seem like it would be
a fitting visit without. (Tho' I think my ever-delayed visit may be
postponed even longer—no point in visiting an historic locale such
as the French Quarter w/o indulging in its rich decadent history!)
and what is it the pirates used to say? "So let's drink and be merry,
for tomorrow we may die." Or was it "so eat, drink and be merry...?"
either way, I see their point. Get it while the getting's good—tomorrow
there might be nothin' left! And judging by the chaos New Orleans
has endured, I'd say they've got a right. So cheers to them!*

And yes, let's keep the correspondence going—I still prefer letters to email, as you have the chance to tuck in little extras, drawings and the like (not too many little extras around here at the moment tho'). But I can't say for sure when I'll get all caught up—it'll be something like six months of email and messages to wade through when I do get out!

Yrs.

Wed, Thur, October 17-18, 2012

A day of struggle. Twin back in action, but his folder still "out". Mine too. After two more rounds of Objective B, mine was pulled as well—for unspecified "bad indicators". Here's where it gets good. "They" say there is no right or single answer they're looking for; that you should be open and honest, not fake any indicators; and you can say anything at all to the examiner. All false. Unless you apply the dictionary definitions to the context of the exercise, in terms of your life and potential case gain, show "very good indictors," and don't ask the wrong questions, you will be punished by being made to go through the same up-to-two-hour drill over and over and/or by having your folder sent away to the case supervisor for interminable "review" further delaying your program. This from speaking to the supe and the examiner over the course of the day. Again, the emphasis being on learning to say what they want you to say over simply learning. And now somebody's having a breakdown three doors down, the sauna having activated some sort of condition, which was loudly described to the objectives room by Mr. Student of the Week. People.

But on the plus side! Finished Larsson's *The Girl who kicked the Hornet's Nest* and there's a new koi in the waterfall pond out in the corner of the parking lot.

Saturday, October 20, 2012

Not a bad day. The cold is receding, after only about three or four days; we've started moving forward a bit better in Objectives—which is a good thing, because I was ready to bail. Had my speech to staff all ready and everything. The roommate's walked out of the course already—was all ready to go home and everything. Decided to stay, and right away started fucking up again with the staff. Got a sexy postcard from Bonnie, she's still looking for apartments for me—the sweetheart! Tomorrow's Sunday, my turn for the easy (non-bathroom) part of room cleaning, and then an hour or so of campus work and it's art, reading and a nap for the rest (I hope). Oh yeah, our morning chore was even cut short because they'd locked all the fucking doors to the course rooms! So just did the bathrooms, hall, and bailed. One staff came by later, when I had to come back for a piss and a wash, but even she couldn't get in—HAH! So, yeah, so far a pretty good day, and just a day ago I wanted to be half-dead on my bathroom floor again...

To Tom fm Joe

Tom,

Your letter writing shows that your overall attitude seems to keep improving. Wow, I don't know if I'll know how to deal with you in a positive (ok maybe semi-positive) frame of mind. Keep working on the art whenever you can. You were missed at the paper-hanging nightmare in Glendale, but not to worry, there'll be another chance in March.

Talk to you soon.

Joe

THE REHABILITATION OF THOMAS MARK

To Tom fm Margaret

Dear Tom,

Congrats on getting through book 4. So, what sorts of communication and perception skills are you being taught? And what sorts of objective exercises are we talking about?

Several years ago, I was in the grocery store on a Saturday (which is unusual for me) and seemed to be running into everyone I knew and was having a great time chatting with folks, etc. I was nearly finished with my list when an older woman I didn't know made some passing remark to me. Normally, I would have pretended I didn't hear her or would have had my iPod on and actually wouldn't have heard her, but I was having such a nice trip, I said something back to her. Thus, a very awkward (on her part) conversation started. Doing what I do for a living, I figured she must be in some sort of therapy and had been given the assignment of striking up a conversation with a stranger. At some point she asked where I lived... I was vague. (I have a healthy dose of paranoia.) And she asked where I attended church (a perfectly acceptable question in the South) and she was mortified to hear me say "Oh, I don't go to church." Then, she pulled a Mary Kay Cosmetics flyer out of her purse and asked me if I would be interested in buying makeup from her... And she was EVEN MORE MORTIFIED when I told her that I didn't wear makeup. She scuttled away from me quickly after that.

I'm kinda imagining a field trip of folks from your facility being dropped off at the mall with the instructions to interact with people.

We've made our Christmas reservations for NOLA already. We are staying in a hotel called Place de Armes and it's just off Jackson Square and next to the cathedral. We are going with a friend, Wendy. Wendy is the most innocent person on the planet... Almost to the point of being totally annoying, almost. I promised that I'd attend midnight mass at the cathedral.

I have hundreds of pictures of the cathedral. I must have been a catholic in a past life.

Love you.

Wednesday, October 24, 2012

A day of challenge—as always. Woke up a couple times in the night, including one around 4:00—and tossed around until almost 6:00. Decided to fuck the "up at 6:00" ethic, and slept 'til 7:00, getting that much needed extra hour. The paper was there, bagged and untouched in the light rain. Alright. There was coffee made, and although they've decided, apparently, to stop stocking the stevia sugar substitute (which you could actually measure, two packets ought to do it, and it dissolved w/o stirring). There was plenty of sugar, so, it was okay. Wolfed the breakfast sammich, and the honeydew, a rare treat, on the fruit platter was sweet and ripe. So, there was that. Peeped in the window of Ethics at the chit board, and because of the bad light I <u>could not tell</u> if I had a chit or not. Afternoon break yielded mail—a surprise package from Joe, *In Extremis: Death and Life in 21st Century Haitian Art*, from the recent Fowler Museum exhibit. Nice! Loads of images and ideas. Turned out I didn't have a chit, and although through dinner break and fourth period I was quitting-time depressed, the fact that I may have pulled off the pass on Objective F (only the sixth book after ten or eleven days) helped immensely. Time to read, write, and keep sketching and jotting down ideas like I have been for the past week. Still not smoking, and the extra oxygen in the lungs and brain seems to be helping the cells.

Friday, October 26, 2012

Kind of a lousy day. Fucking getting keelhauled on Objectives, it's been two goddamn weeks and I'm still only on G#7 of IS and just had the worst costume contest experience ever: only the staff gets to dress up, students have to sit through the parade and vote, after sitting through the clap-fest, then sit through the tabulation of results by the "popular kids" and then the winners, of the staff, are announced. Nobody gets prizes, and there is no candy.

Monday, October 29, 2012—Full moon

A very interesting day, to say the least. But first, Sunday: Almost two hours of chores, then mostly reading, drawing and even a nap! In the evening, after some baseball event that stretched until 9:00 PM, another student put on *Prometheus*, Ridley Scott's so-called "prequel" to the epic *Alien*, which I had seen in theaters but was most unimpressed by. Wanted to give it another chance, as there was a significant factor obscuring the first viewing (alcohol might have been involved).

At any rate, Monday: up and at 'em. Found to my relief that I had passed Objective I, so did J, and then... had the next two periods off, as my twin had a "corneal abrasion". Managed to pass and be able to run on K during last period, enjoyed it and had a fairly good session with the examiner after. The Monday night joy division assembly they call muster was varied by the acoustic guitar and singing of a staff member, with mandatory attendance, of course, and after a long milky warm-up the less-than-delightful attempt at getting a singalong/clapalong going, and then...

It was rather late in the evening, and when the roommate got in I asked him what the deal was with his objectives, if he was being kept in a holding pattern or what. (He hadn't been on course for days.) No, he said; he was going home tomorrow morning. Many matters he needed to deal with, none of which he could handle here, he'd gotten all he could out of the program under its conditions, and it was enough. But that was only the tip of it: the largest of the "matters" to deal with was what he called "spiritual phenomena," which he had been experiencing for years. When I asked him what he meant by "spiritual phenomena" he said he saw visions and heard voices, from the spirit world, which was real. And he readily admitted that this could really be diagnosed as symptoms of schizophrenia. It all started, apparently, around ten years ago, when dealing with a cocaine addiction, in a search for guidance he fell under the spell of a "Satanist practicing under the guise of Divinity," or some such thing, a liar from the divine/world/grace/something or other. And while he had been "graced" with two months reprieve here at Oakview, these visitations had returned regularly in the middle of the night... So, long and short, for three months I've been sharing a room with a mentally ill person twice my size...

Wednesday, October 31, 2012—Halloween

An interesting day. Up at 6:30, the room all my own for the time being. Paper a-waiting, had the simple breakfast then enjoyed a leisurely shower, shampoo and shave. It was mentioned that Mohammed, an older Indian (?) gent from St. Louis might be moving into the room; this apparently suggested to him by the IC and seconded by another neighbor here in the ghetto to stave off the possibility of Mohammed's roommate "Twitch" from moving in—he of the crack pipe, constant spastic motions (apparently at all hours) and running internal monolog complete with spontaneous outbursts of "son of a bitch!" and "fucking whore!" So that would be all right. "Mo" is a pretty upbeat guy. Got the morning chore out of the way, speaking to Mo in the process while getting supplies (nice fog this morning, by the way—and a full moon as well!), and he confirmed he has submitted the request to move in. Marcus and I got him through a couple Objectives and I took a stab at L again. And what do you know, fourth period was replaced by the pumpkin carving contest! Can't remember if I listed my ideas already, but:

"Pumpkins must be appropriate" reads the joy-killer qualifier in small print at the bottom of the flyer. And my top ideas were, if not completely inappropriate, definitely material for high-level frowns:

1. Great Pumpkin triumph of the will: Satire (cross between Leni Riefenstahl's *Triumph of the Will* and Schulz's *Peanuts*, with a double row of pumpkins running up the building and front stairs toward a larger, "great" pumpkin. All of the smaller ones with swastikas carved into them and a lighted candle inside —"inappropriate" and unfeasible.

2. Classic "passed-out-with-a-dick-drawn-on-his-face" — "inappropriate."

3. L. Ron Hubbard (Squash)—frowned upon, no doubt.

4. Dias de los Muertos painted skull design—too intricate; couldn't be done in the ninety-minute fourth period course, even if it could, wouldn't have a picture of it after.

5. Suicide protest pumpkin: just smashed on the ground, with a roadside shrine-style candle memorial—conceptual; frowned upon, no doubt.

I decided not to participate, for the above reasons plus the fact that we would most likely not be able to boil, bake, and eat the seeds (half the fun of the carving anyway), and, AND, all non-participants had to go to "course" –nothing like mandatory participation to kill the joy of holiday fun. "Heil Halloween!" But the course "option" was removed and Marcus and I found ourselves with little choice. Having prepared for nothing more than the busywork of "clearing" words for an hour-and-a-half, we now had a pumpkin. (Marcus asked one of the staff if this was really mandatory; the reply was, "Well, we're not going to make you have a good time..." "No," I said, "you're not.") Marcus was about to stage a sit-out, but I went with the conceptual no-effort minimal participation plan: throw the pumpkin in a clear plastic bin-bag and dumped it in a corner of the porch outside.

To Tom fm Dad

Hi ya Tom,

Halloween here—and there too I suppose. Don't know if there'll be any trick or treaters out this way, but have a little candy just in case.

Back to Portland weather. Rain everyday now, nearly all day. Haven't biked or run outdoors since coming back from Berlin. Nice to have a bike and treadmill in the spare room.

Haven't heard from you in a while, hope all is going okay there. Have they let you out for a movie or anything? I'm watching the first season of the <u>Deadwood</u> HBO series. Took a couple issues to get into it but enjoying it now. Nothing other than that.

Take care.

Love,
Dad

To Tom fm Margaret

Dear Tom,

Howdy. When I sent your last letter, I'd just sealed it up when I saw some reference to snow in Lake Tahoe. I thought your facility was in/near/next to Lake Tahoe. I was jealous for a few minutes when I thought you were getting snow and we weren't. I love snow. It makes me inexplicably happy.

We saw little more than wind from Sandy. Over the weekend, we were visiting friends who live in the Northeast corner of NC, they had rain (not terribly heavy) and wind, but nothing like what we typically see from hurricanes and tropical storms.

We have a new employee in our office. YAY! And, I got the treat of being able to hire from our volunteer/former intern pool. It is rare that we have a position open up when we have a recent intern looking for work. And, we have a new Thai restaurant in town. So, life is looking up, right?

How is your supply of snack foods? Any requests?

Prehab 2011

Spring, 2011

What the fuck did I do today...

drank coffee, smoked cigarettes
updated résumé and cover letter (a little—fairly good shape,
I think)
looked online for work: applied for quality assurance
position w/Volt
read some Bukowski stories
took out mail
bought:

    newspaper (nothing worth clipping or applying for)
    lottery ticket (HA! But $125 M worth gambling on)
    flints for Elvis zippo (and installed)
    cigarettes

paid bills
called Office Team, set up appointment for Wednesday to
"re-up" for temp positions
worked on "sleep" drawing
made list for Cuban-style black bean stew (smoky and hot;
will add potatoes and sausage this time) will shop tomorrow
chatted briefly with neighbor (still don't know his name; was
drunk when we met months ago)
completed first major round of shredding outdated
documents
screened/reviewed older CDs for sale pile
checked email (nothing worth mentioning)
took a shit
played with banjo, with help of *Banjo for Dummies* book
did some research and sketching for Ganesh piece
cleaned the pipes (meaning jerked off)
washed dishes (meaning washed dishes)
did some minor exercises (light lifting, crunches)

Got a call from Scott Peterson, at BHI, he wants to take me over to the shop to meet with Tareq and discuss using some of my designs for t-shirts. Maybe some existing, maybe a custom original. Yes! Would be great to get some scratch, as well as get back into the publishing underground. Scotty from Bounty Hunter picked me up at 12:30 PM, and we went over to the shop. Saw the owner, Tareq, again, interesting guy, and met Chris and Alex who work the print side of the place. Hung out for a couple hours shooting the shit, noting the poor plagiaristic state of what used to be the underground. Got many positive words on the folder of drawings I brought along, as well as for *Malefact*; they expressed interest in many of my pieces, indicating they're just going to have trouble narrowing it down to a manageable number. No cash was discussed, but agreements all round that interest is maintained and will move forward. Oh yeah, Tareq brought lunch—Mexican food, didn't have to eat the rest of the day. Got dropped off, no bills in the mailbox—woo-hoo!

Went online, received instructions for meeting at Office Team, did the online registration update thing. Found my way to the office of Robert Half International (Office Team), west of Ocean at the corner of Ocean and Daisy. Met with Danielle Thomas after filling out some forms: interview went fairly well. Marked "yes" for misdemeanors for 1986 hit and run—now they'll have to run a background check, with "long", "messy" forms. Danielle didn't anticipate a problem. Went home and changed out of the suit, looked rather sharp if I do say so myself. Felt depressed for some reason; thought about drink, thought about suicide. Took a piss, had a peanut butter and chipotle power sandwich, had a cup of tea and a cigarette. Watched some TV, went to bed early.

Danielle from Office Team called. She may have found a short-term placement for me at a property management company here in Long Beach. It would be primarily analysis and reporting of claim situations. The company hasn't yet received final approval for temporary hiring, but according to

Danielle they need someone badly. And I still need to receive and complete the "data sheet" required for the background check. But all in all, things look promising, if not guaranteed, on the work-front, both personally and professionally. "It's a good thing."

Got a notice from my health insurance company in the mail. The claim from my last hospital stay has been delayed pending "internal review". So, that's a bill of $60,308.17 still floating out there. Maybe right over my head. And then I tried calling the hot bartender, Shannon, from Clancy's. She's a good-looking tattooed motorcycle riding stencil artist who gets high, drinks, and can hold a conversation. She gave me her number and agreed to go to dinner with me, and although I did get ahold of her once (so I know it's her real number) she started dodging and not returning my calls. So I figure dinner was off, but she still has my *Texas Chain Saw Massacre* remake DVD, and I do want that back. After letting it ride for a while I gave her a call tonight, but her number now dials to the mailbox of some guy with a Japanese sounding name. So she either moved, died, or changed her number. In any event, that DVD is a write-off. Do some more inking, read the paper, try the crosswords, watch some TV, sit here by myself saying "fuck" a lot.

Lately I've been getting very low and rundown in the evenings, starting in the afternoon. Early afternoon. Maybe it's getting up too early and drinking too many sugared coffees, but depression is fairly constant. Today no exception. Had a pretty good start, did some research and sketching while some flicks were on, even caught the Three Stooges on the tube. Did some writing and typing, sorted out a couple more CDs, did some shredding and dishwashing... scanning... but I get tired. Craving the escape of drink and dope, even though they don't really help. And I can never get enough sleep. Feel that past efforts have never been enough; making future efforts seem pointless. Been alone so long now I almost feel that I have nothing to offer any more. Wish I had someone to talk to, or to see, but I don't, not really. Need more regular encouragement and kindness. Again the train of thought that there's really nothing that I want to do anymore. I can escape into books for a while, but even that gets tiring. Don't know what to do. So tired. So tired.

> Now I lay me down to sleep
> Where I can fly and never weep
> Please let me die before I wake
> Nevermore mistakes to make.

Worked on mandala design motif for sleep drawing, and think I fixed the floral titty-tatts I fucked up before. Went to the bank, moved some $ from savings to checking, took out some cash. Still have $11.8K in the bank, $450 in cash, $25K credit limit on two cards, thinking of traveling. Worked with the banjo (that was a nice thing), learned some chords (G, D?, C) and practiced fingering. Called Office Team, spoke to Danielle who confirmed that all is underway/in-order. The background check has come back, but it went straight to legal for review. So, maybe another seventy-two hours or so. Possible position still open at property management office, they haven't confirmed hiring yet. Said she had another opportunity come across her desk... as a trust administrator... at Wells Fargo! D'oh! Maybe another time... Reading and enjoying *Beneath the Moors* by Brian Lumley, *Blue of Noon* by Georges Bataille, and *Czar!* By Larry ("Leatherman") Townsend.

Banged away at Grandmother's hands, finished up (after weeks) and took it over to make copies and mail to Margaret. It's the only thing she's ever asked of me.

Talked briefly to the neighbor lady in Apt. G, Vivian. She's a grandmother, and runs a cleaning company. According to Mr. Fowler, who lives below her, she's noisy as hell, and a couple other neighbors have said she's kind of odd (including the indication she may be "on something"), but she's always been nice enough to me.

Got invited to a BBQ at Celia's, went over, joined her, Johnny, Lisa, Bill, his date Jose, Celia's friend Tona (who I think I hit on previously more than once when loaded), and Celia's step brother Vern. All nice people, good time, good food, but I definitely felt out of my element. A different set of tastes and backgrounds. Plus everyone else was drinking and getting high, so I was on another wavelength entirely. Hard to carry on a conversation when everyone's wasted and out of it. Went home feeling kind of sad. Always so fucking hard to communicate. Did not sleep well, hard to get to sleep, then woke up at 3:00 AM unable to get back to sleep until 5:00 AM.

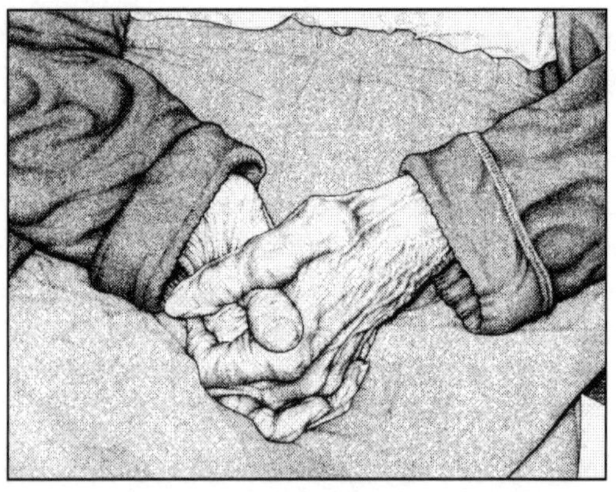

Spent the weekend with Joe and Bonnie. On the way home conversation came round to the events of the last year. And with a very reasonable train of thought and some rational good humor, they managed, without being at all judgmental, to impress upon me how much my alcoholism and suicidal behavior had been impacting my friends, neighbors and family. Something which I had recognized a very little bit on one level, yet had chosen for the most part to ignore. A good talk: everybody now seems much happier with the current path and condition. We will see where things go. I should, and would like to, talk to Lisa and Johnny, and Celia, and not only express my apologies for causing undue grief and concern, but simply to say "thank you for giving a shit".

Kind of shitty mood today. Started with the alarm at 6:30 so I could get up and go to the dentist to get the left half of the mouth done. Deep scaling upper and lower. Had Candy today, and although she used more anesthetic than either of the other two techs it was still much more uncomfortable on the upper and lower, both with the scraping and the ultrasound. My teeth still hurt. No mail at PO Box or at home. Thinking shitty thoughts about work and money, about people, took a catnap, did some inking, still just want to blank out.

Was awakened at 1:30 AM by the party boys next door. Went over and asked them to keep it down, received apology and they shut the music off—but now I was awake. Got up, sat around then made coffee and did some inking. Left a message for Danielle at Office Team, then logged onto the computer and found an email from a lady at the *Examiner* saying "we have reviewed your application and think you would make an excellent <u>Long Beach Ethnic Food Examiner</u> (in our Food and Drink channel)"! Working on that response now. Established a PayPal account, I think, although "Examiner.com makes no guarantee as to minimum payment." Basically you write pieces for your topic, and then get paid based on the number of readers you attract. Which you're supposed to go to "social networking" sites and promote the *Examiner* and try to attract advertisers and other reviewers for the *Examiner.* Big scam (not even any promotional items offered—you have to come up with and provide your own shit). But ought to help tailor the writing to the "mainstream" and be a résumé enhancer. Anyway, that whole process, signing up for PayPal, preparing the bio and bio photo, etc., took about five hours, largely because goddamn McAfee decided to update the security center at that time. But got that done, sent out the email. And then it was 9:00 PM. Fuck me. Long day.

Three months today without drinking. Didn't even leave the

apartment. Up around 5:00-5:30 AM, worked all day. Inking, typing, editing, internet research. Uninstalled the goddamn delay-causing Google toolbar that got installed with the Flash player. Got two months of job possibilities from Office Team, neither of which look like they will work. One is a medical claims processing, reporting gig, elementary skills and responsibilities

for which I would be great at, but don't have the "prior claims processing with knowledge of stop loss contracts and self-funded plans" required, or "medical coding background". The other, which Danielle was almost embarrassed to offer, was a trucking company, handling reports, field calls and custdmer complaints, very high-stress, high-volume, people yelling and cursing at you all day, for $12.06/hr, maybe $15.00 if it goes full time, but where do you go from there? Dispatcher? Like I told her, I appreciate the thought and mention, but was really looking for a temp-to-hire position I could grow into. Not much room to move as a phone jockey for a truck stop. I submitted another article to Examiner.com (Mom's Specialty Mediterranean). McAfee kicked in with the download/install and locked everything up. I'm just about finished with the "sleep" drawing, just need to decide whether to add one further detail, took a lot of work and I'm not sure I'm pleased with it.

Summer, 2011

Been working this week for California Credits Group, at the Renaissance Hotel downtown. One of those big ritzy places right on the main drag. Arched driveway entrance, grand glass waterfall behind the bar stocked with $300 colored decanters, free newspapers, "class all around". I was down in the guts of the inn, going through confidential personnel files, pulling tax and employment data for scanning. All day, in the basement. Only perk is peering through the disciplinary action reports. Theft, sexual harassment, illegal alien status, the ruination of Mr. Jong's birthday party... It was all poorly written, much of it in Spanish, but it was evident that it's always a grand time at the old four-star. Sucks, but like I've been saying all week, it's more money than I would have made sitting around the house. And it's only a week. In a bad and uncertain mood all evening. Caught a glimpse of myself while waiting in the lobby this morning and was reminded of what an ugly son of a bitch I am, on top of everything else. I just cannot wait for the next good excuse to hit the downward spiral again.

Didn't open the front door all day today. Thought about fetching the paper, but didn't really need one, and it was raining. Worked on the inking, added an article to Examiner.

com (Chicharrene Chaparrar: round five—Elena's Original Chicharon). Added some shit to Facebook, checked the Office Team site for jobs (not shit in Long Beach). Did a little research and started an article on black mirror meditation; I'd made a black mirror, usually used for scrying, years ago (I think I saw it referenced in Burroughs) but never tried it; used it yesterday, and it was actually pretty eye-opening; actually saw images or visions, the way you might in clouds or in a dream state, and came away with a relaxed feeling of clarity. Going to have to do more of that. Called Karen in Portland, girlfriend from something like twenty years ago who reconnected with me on Facebook—don't know if that'll turn out to be a good idea or not. A friend of Justin's from Isla Vista, Kirsten's too. Very awkward conversation. Long pauses.

I ride the bus. Owning a car is a big pain in the ass for me, what with maintenance, parking, parking tickets, gas and oil prices, licensing, registration and insurance, road rage, toll booths, traffic jams, traffic tickets, taxes, tags and emissions tests, long lines of brilliance at the DMV, car washes, flat tires, battery death, shifty mechanics, shifty salesmen, carless assholes bumming rides, tow truck drivers lifting your ride, drunken driving, theft, vandalism and parking lot hit and runs—you name it, I don't want it.

Not to mention that fact that most people just drive like shit. Put a frustrated halfwit with a hangover and a nagging wife behind the wheel of a ton of steel and just watch how he reacts when his chickpea brain thinks his lane position is being threatened. Or those geniuses in middle management who aren't important enough to have a driver, but are so important that they need to be on their cell phone every minute of their commute and simply can't be concerned with the color of the traffic light. Women doing their makeup with both hands. Slobs stuffing fast-food breakfasts into their faces with both hands. Pimple-dicks looking for a drag race at every stop sign. You see it every day. Then, you go home and see the results on the evening news. There ought to be a betting pool. So I take the bus.

But you're paying for more than your ride. Oh yes. It's not always an adventure, but sometimes it comes damn close. Junkies, psychos, common criminals, people who change their babies right there on the seat, they all take the bus. Just not on any regular schedule. When they do they're always on the verge of an argument or an overdose that would, most likely, be very much worth the brief delay. "Sorry I'm late—our bus driver got stabbed in the face when he stopped to kick off a junkie who puked on the floor." Just listening to some of these Nobel winners' rich conversations is more than worth the price of admission. Bi-polar childhood casualties trying to impress one another. Juvenile 'gangstas' doing the same (if you're such a hustler, why are you still riding the bus?). Ex-con speed freaks having a conversation with themselves, just daring someone else to join in. The hopeless. The doomed. And you.

Don't forget the ones who make it a point of honor never to pay for a ride. They'll take all day, and a chunk of yours, getting kicked off of bus after bus just so they don't have to pay the fare. Shit, man, it's a dollar for a ride and a transfer; if you can't afford that, chances are good a free bus ride ain't gonna improve your life anyway. It's just like those cheap cunts who spend twenty minutes hunched over staring into the newspaper box, reading as much of the paper as they can for free. Buddy, if you can't afford twenty-five cents there's nothing in there you need to know.

And then there are the ones who sit next to you. Your ideal seat partner will be slim, quiet and clean-smelling—and there simply are not enough people like that in the world, let alone riding the bus and sitting next to you. No, you'll draw the prize pig every time. The ones who stink of cancer and bad teeth. The ones sweating out a lifetime of cheap liquor and bad luck as they slump across the seat. The ones just released (or escaped) from one institution or another and still working the meds out of their system. The ones who shit their pants in warm weather. The homeless. (Hey, are those lice?) It's true; the people on the bus who talk to you are never the ones you want to be talking to. To the pretty airline stewardess you're nothing but a lump of shit in a suit jacket, but to the elderly and infirm you're a truly magnetic individual. No peace for you—you can just close up your book of Hammett or Celine and put it away. It's time to hear about Granny's colonoscopy! Actually it's rarely anything that interesting—she just wants somebody to bounce bus routes off of as she explains, in great detail, how difficult it is to get back and forth from the medical center in West L.A. Suggesting she pick up a bus schedule will do no good—the old bag is dead set on having some company, and you're the lucky man. It's only two miles to your stop, not too far to get off and walk...

Another joy of bussing is the chance your lungs have to swim around in the same air as everybody else's. In the best of times those commuter cans are hotboxes of influenza; right after the latest CDC report, well, you just hope you stay lucky. Somebody coughs harshly in the back. Oh shit, Tuberculosis! The Chinese girl across the aisle sneezes. Asian Bird Flu! Hanta Virus! West Nile! Dengue Fever! AIRBORNE ENCEPHALITIS! And hey man, what the fuck is that sticky shit all over the handlebar and seat back, anyway? And always, always, from somewhere, the faint smell of dead animals. It's like a boxcar to Bergen-Belsen—packed in too tightly to move, headed someplace you really don't want to go. Me and Bugs Bunny—"OOOO-oo! I'm DIE-in'!!!"

Riding the bus gives you just enough time to think about these things.

My next placement was at a vitamin factory. Or, more accurately, a 'health food supplement manufacturer.' They needed a monkey to man the phones and plug the BRCs (Business Reply Cards) into their database while the company was in the process of shedding its skin and transitioning to another state. Guess the tax breaks were better in the gambling states than they were in California. The company was called Health Aids or, more unfortunately, Health AIDS after their primary product, a free radical-fighting compound promising "Advanced Implementation of Detoxification Systematization." They made other shit too.

After about a week I was told to change desks. I was moved into the Black Ladies' Office, set down between another temp, Ned, and an office veteran, Nettie. I didn't mind, but I didn't think it bade well for me when the first thing the division director did after moving me in was to tell Nettie to turn off her radio. They weren't happy. But at least they didn't openly take it out on me. They just cranked it back up when the department head wasn't around.

Over some R. Kelly, Nettie asked me if the radio was too loud. I said it was fine. I didn't really relish the prospect of listening to Kelly and Fat Joe for eight hours a day, but I'd be goddamned if I was going to tell a sixty-year-old black woman who said "motherfucker" as much as she did to turn off her music. That broad looked as strong as a horse—she'd probably kick me right down the fucking stairs. Nettie was all right, though. With the imminent closing of the office her attitude was, "We all fuckin' temps now," the unspoken deal being that as long as I took care of my shit and didn't give her any grief everything would be fine.

When Nettie found out I'd never actually sampled the products I'd been hawking all day long she asked me if I wanted to try some. "Sure." "What flavor you like? Strawberry? Banana?" "Sure, strawberry-banana would be fine." That was another one of their flavors. Nettie went down to the warehouse for a couple minutes. "Here you go!" She dumped three one-pound cans of high-vitamin energy drink mix on my desk. "Damn! Thanks Nettie." "You hold on, I'll get you some more." Next time she was out of the office Nettie came back with another couple of cans, along with a boxful of single-serving packets. "That oughta hold you!" I started making coffee in the morning after that.

Not only did I not feel suicidally defeated when I got home, sometimes I was actually in a good mood. After ten-and-a-half hours of commuting and customer service. Well I'll be—I must have brain cancer after all.

The cavalier attitude, which I'd often adopted in the past, was a sort of, "It's a temp job, fuck it, who cares." Unfortunately I had to care. The piss-poor pay rate of this gig, coupled with the fact that it was the first assignment with this agency, made it pretty clear that in order to score another, higher-paying, placement, I had to care. Had to make a good impression, get a good report card, get a good referral for the next gig. Work hard, get along, and, in essence, suck up but good. So I did. I institutionalize remarkably well. My phone manner was acceptable, my processing speed quick for a newbie, and I was one pleasant motherfucker no matter how tired or hungover I was on any particular day. I knew my place. Hired geek. Lowest step on the way to the porta-shitter. Maggot. If any shit came up I was well and truly fucked, disposable on all fronts. I wouldn't be missed

And it paid off. On Monday of the last week Nikki didn't come in. We were told that she wouldn't be in all week. I guess her spending half the day online looking for a better job didn't go over real well with the boss. That, or the fact that she was able to accomplish less than half the work of everybody else in between snacks (build that ass!), break time, and vigorous whining about how boring the job was. (She did have a good line for a particular type of all-too-frequent caller though: "STUPID!") Even Nettie, who I'd come to know as a woman of exceedingly good humor, was glad to see her go. "Homegirl was workin' on my very last nerve," she said, sounding like she meant it. It was a shame; now I'd not only have to answer all of those goddamn phone calls myself, but I'd miss the titty shot she gave me several times a day when she leaned back over my desk for a back stretch. Oh well.

The company had pushed back their closure date by a week, but people continued to drift away at a steady rate. Rats leaving the sinking ship; even the Tin Cats were empty. Now it was just me and the stragglers who hadn't moved, moved on, quit without notice, or were counting the days until they could file for unemployment and take a state-sanctioned vacation. Some employees had their departure noted (at least the office bought hamburgers for everybody rather than cake); some made the rounds on their way out. (What the hell are you hugging me for?! You've been here eight years, I've been here two weeks!) The managers were in and out of the office, flying back and forth to hire and train new help out-of-state, and everybody else really seemed to be looking forward to the place folding. People had been carrying bagloads of shit out of the warehouse and office suite all week, and by the last day they were even tearing the clocks off the walls and hauling those away as well.

And that was the end of that assignment. In the immortal words of back-biting sportscaster Marv Albert, "YES!!!"

Finished the article on Nangustoon juice for Examiner.com. Did some more inking. Really wound up today, angry, tense, maybe it was waking up at 4:30 AM to empty the fucking sink. Hit the grocery store, picked up some beer and Black Velvet, had a couple, then called Chris and went down to Hayden to have a couple more and spend too much money. Chatted and joked with the bar folk, swapped rounds, then back here for a late night hot dog run to 7-11.

Fall, 2011

Since the last period of sobriety, I willfully underwent a heavy period of an overdose on alcohol and cigarettes (raspberry Smirnoff and Camel Blue, respectably, or is it respectfully?) Anyway after the Black Velvet was such rotgut that it made me vomit, I made the switch. But it got to be too much, so I went cold turkey on both—and had the worst time ever, days of constant vomiting and diarrhea, shivering, shaking, the inability to sleep, and lots of bad thoughts. And this lasted for I don't know how many days. But I finally came out of it today and got busy. Rearranged a few things, fixed the desk lamp I busted up while my Dad was here, picked the place up a bit and paid a couple bills. Took a nap, took the first shower in what must have been weeks, washed the hair. My apartment bathroom is haunted: at all hours of the day and night it sounds like somebody is pissing, flushing and washing their hands. Got online for the first time, as usual I hadn't really been missing anything, although my sister Margaret tells me our grandparents are missing...

It was quite a day; it was quite a day before it was 8:00 AM. Didn't (really) sleep at all last night. Got up, dicked around, watched TV, drank Gatorade. Finished shaving off the rest of the beard (kept the sideburns, as always). Did some dishes, until it was time to go to the hospital. I'd actually made the mistake of calling them and asking if I could talk to somebody about the tiny teeth that had appeared on my lower lip... and this from somebody who's completely sober... for the moment... anyhow, I'd been told that I'd be seeing a female doctor, so I did the psycho thing and shaved off my beard (which really needed to go anyway), thinking like a fool, "oh boy—I get to meet me a hot doctor!"

I was told that I'd have an 8:00 AM appointment (I have an idea why I was given an appointment so quickly!) and to show up by 7:45; but I got there earlier than that, despite walking, and had to wait in the growing heat. Got in, filled out the forms, and was led by a nurse into a waiting room. After a couple minutes the doctor arrived: a large bald black man. He was a nice enough guy, but not at all what I was expecting.

Anyway he asked me a lot of drug questions, for good reason, and we got along okay. Got my weight taken, and it came out 127—more or less ten pounds lighter than when I last weighed myself. No wonder I'm hallucinating. I'd called the hospital because of the tiny teeth, but as long as I was there I had other complaints that I was hoping they could help me with: the painful greenish coating that no matter how hard I try I just cannot get rid of; the insomnia; the numbness of my feet. Got signed up for three different tests, all of which involved drawing blood, so I got three vials of that drawn, grabbed a pink grapefruit lollipop, drank a lot of water and headed home.

Been working at eating more so I can stand up and get around and not fall down so much. Tried to hang myself the other day, but my buddy Joe was right; the noose hanging from the doorframe was too low. I thought if I just let my weight take over it would work, but if your feet can touch the floor you automatically go up on your toes. I was standing on a chair in the living room trying to screw the noose into the higher ceiling when the phone rang, for some reason I got down to answer it. There was no immediate answer, indicating it was a telemarketer or one of those auto-dialer deals, so I hung up and instead of getting back up on the chair I called the old man. Dad came out for a few days and we actually had a pretty damn good time. Played cards, did some talking, went out to eat, went to see *Capitan America: the First Avenger*, which was pretty fucking good, went to the roller derby at the Queen Mary Dome (Bixby Rollerettes vs. Belmont Hot Broads), went to the Aquarium of the Pacific which had loads of crazy underwater animals, invertebrates and mammals alike.

I'll probably be going up to S.F. for a while. Ought to be a good change of pace for a month or two. Although I was stricken with the horrible notion that the whole offer of San Francisco is nothing other than a trick to pull me into some sort of program or intervention... Feel pathetic and weak. I'm essentially moving back home for a short while because I can't take care of myself. Rather, not so much that I can't, I simply won't take proper responsibility. Maybe the change of pace (?) and scenery will do me good. Ate dinner, and started freaking out. No job and no girl is bad enough, but my PC is dying, my refrigerator is dying, although my credit is good I still have more debt than money in the bank, I wasted that $100K I got from Fran's death, I've got the shakes, my memory is gone, I have no inspiration, there's a lump in my throat, and I feel bad about everything and everyone all of the time. I just want it to be over. I need a drink and a cigarette.

San Francisco, 2011

San Francisco. Shit. I hadn't been to the place in years. And while I used to live there, and in surrounding areas, the truth is I really didn't miss it very much. The constant crime, high prices and never-ending stink of piss just weren't much in the way of selling points. Despite all of that, this metropolis of modern Sodom really is a gorgeous city.

We made the pilgrimage from L.A. County up north to Fog City USA. We took the 405, which, while not as scenic as the Oceanside 1, had the dual advantages of being quicker and not requiring us to concern ourselves with avoiding mudslides and falling rocks. Pretty smooth sailing, if not the most picturesque; we drove past power yards and RV lots, office blocks and shopping centers, warehouses and new housing developments that looked almost medieval in the way they crammed an unbelievable amount of wage-slave peasants into cookie-cutter units. "EVILL" (sic) spray-painted on an overpass. Trucks hauling Putzmeister cranes. Some cat on horseback riding down a busy street in the rain. All of this while still within Los Angeles County.

And then the hills, alternately lush and verdant or scarred and vacant, all just waiting to catch fire again. By the time the 405 runs into the 5 things get really interesting. ("Is that sarcasm? That's my least favorite thing, sarcasm.") The hills level out and get smaller and bleaker (well, not so small that you don't see the occasional falling rock sign—guess we do have to look out for those after all), and by the time you approach Bakersfield you're in the flat fields. Cattle grazing, fruit and shit growing in orchards on either side (adorned with what I suspect were bat houses, like birdhouses but built and raised for the nocturnal mammals in order that they might aid pollination), migrants dressed like firefighters harvesting the road shoulders for recyclables, the occasional humping oil derrick. Lots of brown unused land as well; apparently the local growers are having their water rationed, getting wrung a little dryer every year as an increasing volume of water is channeled to metropolitan areas. "No Water No Food" signs were frequently spotted, more foreboding than any scarecrow.

Passed Pleasant Valley State Prison (home of flower arranging and mess hall date rape?), feedlots, rows of beehives, and "$1000 Fine for Littering" signs surrounded by empty beer bottles before cruising through Altamont Pass and its fleet of giant windmills rising up from the surrounding hills.

Drove past the hellhole where I spent far too many of my formative years, Livermore, home of the secretive Lawrence Livermore National Laboratory ('The Lab'). A tiny shithole of a "city" that seemed (when I lived there, anyway) composed of equal parts eggheads, ranchers, Cholos and drugged-out white trash, this little cow town was so surreal and unpleasant as to be almost science-fictional. In keeping with the environment, one of our favorite hangouts was the burned-out and abandoned V.A. hospital up in the hills, a massive complex of buildings with the leavings of what we took to be drug-induced satanic rituals and graffiti offering messages such as "Satan is my garbage man" and "I raped my dog." Genius. Not the best place to take a date, but if you wanted to get loaded, hunt for discarded medical equipment and play ditch-the-police, it was as good a spot as any.

Beyond that, Oakland. I lived in Oakland for a time as well, in a most disreputable crack house in a state of constant ill repute. It wasn't a 'gangsta' crack house actually, just a rundown shit-level flat where a bunch of guys lived who had more crack cocaine than cash money on hand. Our place was located directly across the street from the psychiatric emergency entrance of Highland Hospital, the place where the Oakland Superintendent of Schools was taken when he was shot by the SLA. We liked to say that the area was so mean that even the neighborhood cats were tougher than shit and definitely creatures not to be messed with, as 'Ol' One-Eye', a big local tomcat who'd lost an eye in an alley fight, used to sodomize my flatmate's male kittens whenever they unwisely stepped outside. But, truthfully, we had very few problems with crime. (Thank fuck.)

Finally we crossed the Bay Bridge into San Francisco, just as the sun was setting, and I have to say that The City does proffer a most beautiful skyline. (But then again, maybe it's just because you can't see all the people from that distance.) That evening we hit up the famous City Lights bookstore on Columbus, where it's far too easy to spend far too much money on everything from fiction to 'Evidence' to sociology and politics (well, not for me maybe, but for you precious student types), before heading down the street to The Stinking Rose ("A Garlic Restaurant") for a stinking good meal. An appetizer of rolls spread with garlic roasted in olive oil and a "hint" of anchovies was a good starter, followed by the forty-clove garlic chicken as an entrée. It all finished off rather nicely with a bowl of garlic ice cream drenched in caramel sauce (a lot better than it sounds—the garlic actually gives the ice cream a 'warm' quality without being overpowering, and the caramel is a surprisingly good match). I think they actually had garlic-flavored condoms available there at one time as well, although I didn't see any on sale this time.

Got up fairly early and headed out to Golden Gate Park with Dad. He went out for a run with his long-standing running group (SFRRC) and I took a stroll through the park. (And why run, if nobody's chasing you? And if your lifestyle is such that you don't have to worry about people chasing you on a regular basis, wouldn't your time be better spent on the firing range?) Looked at the Dutch windmill and flower garden, wandered through the park "exploring" some of the countless paths and little nooks and crannies running through the park. Didn't run into any coyote or homeless, which is probably all right. Stopped in at the Beach Chalet/Park Chalet and grabbed a cup of tea, drank that as I walked along the beach. There was a group of Druids or Wiccans or something circled around a fire on the beach. I took a picture but it didn't come out... well, they may have thwarted my invasion of their privacy (although as Dad pointed out, it was a public space), but they weren't apparently all wise enough to turn off their lights—a number of vehicles in the parking lot were sitting empty with their lights on...

Dinner was much better, in fact the best meal I had in SF. (Also the most expensive, but worth it.) Dosa is an Indian restaurant at 1700 Fillmore that excels on every level. High ceilings, two floors, subtle lighting, good color scheme and excellent décor (the giant wrought iron gateway-style design works used as wall hangings and lit from behind were particularly impressive) all combine to give the place a truly pleasant ambiance. The service is top notch (so long as you have a reservation) and the food is flavorful, elegant, and unique to my experience. We each opted for the Taste of Southern India Signature Four Course Tasting.

The dishes were all on the subtle side (read: small), but you get four of them and they were all mighty fine. And after all of that the restaurant impressed me even further by offering the best hot air hand dryer I've ever seen in a restroom: not only did it actually dry my hands, but it put forth such a mighty gale of hot air that I could see the powerful wind tunnel effect of the thing as it pushed the skin of my hands out like ripples on a pond. Cool. All in all, definitely a good place to keep in mind for date night. (Nice wine selection, too.)

Got up early, had coffee and a cigarette, read the papers. Dad's on an all-day bike ride, so I hoofed it up to Fillmore and went north and south there for a bit. Looked in some markets for pork rinds, but all they stocked were El Sabroso Pork Cracklins, which I'd had before. Did find an interesting Asian Market with all sorts of wild goods, including an extensive collection of deli fresh kimchi. Stopped in at Harry's bar for a spicy Bloody Mary and a brief chat with the bar girls. Went to Bun Mee Vietnamese Sandwich eatery on the way home and picked up a grilled pork sammich, went on home and had half of that with some kimchi and a beer.

The next day we had breakfast at The Grove on Fillmore, a cabin-style restaurant/café featuring exposed rafters, rock (or rock-style) walls, a fireplace, friendly staff and one of the best breakfast burritos I've ever had. And then there was the gigantic beaker of freshly-squeezed orange juice that landed on the table. Apparently the place is quite the hangout for yuppies and students to meet and greet and play with their laptops and cell phones all day, take that as you will.

My night to cook. We hit Mollie Stones and picked up the basics, dropped these off and I hoofed it up to Fillmore and Post to the huge Japanese complex. Took me a minute or two to find the Nijiya Market there, but I got it and they had every item on my list, some of which were rather obscure as far as ordinary grocery stores go. Even got the weirdest bottle of melon soda I'd ever seen to drink on the walk back. Got home and started prepping right away (aided by some samples of rare scotch from the old man's liquor cabinet).

Main course: pork cutlets, marinated in a mixture of: plum sauce, black bean garlic sauce, hoi sin sauce, chili garlic sauce, sweet rice wine vinegar, brown sugar, black pepper. Baked for fifty minutes at 350°, covered, each cutlet topped by a scored plum half that had been soaked in sake.

Up at 7:00 AM, out to Aquatic Park with Dad so he could swim in the Bay and I could take a walk around. Went down the end of the pier to do the tourist thing and take pictures of Alcatraz. Then headed up toward Fort Mason, not much to see there but a large quasi-religious statue/sculpture. A big stone Madonna like figure with a mosaic inlay down near the bottom of a four eyed child-cherub. Walking back to the car I saw some other swimmers, and nearby a number of sea lions were watching them, surfacing and submerging at random. I was waiting to see if one would attack, but although apparently this does happen occasionally when they get territorial, they usually keep their distance. Went to the Buena Vista for breakfast, home of the "world famous" Irish coffee. But on an empty stomach, and with Dad, I passed on that and had grapefruit juice and a Denver omelet instead. A little later we did the other tourist thing and strolled through Fisherman's Wharf, which was a disappointment. Even Cannery Row has been sucked lifeless: gone are the bookstore, scrimshaw shop, Japanese toy store, the place where you could buy those transparent little plastic boxes in a variety of sizes and colors, and other fun places. Now it's almost all office space and family restaurants. Sucks.

Ah well, on to some fucking culture: the famed de Young Museum in Golden Gate Park. Fuck that special limited engagement exhibition of Impressionist paintings on loan from France; I went straight up to the Oceanic and New Guinea art galleries. Fucking amazing they are, with a myriad of carvings from all over the South Pacific. It's all eye-catching and inspiring, and even the more crude works of art and ceremonial ornamentation are impressive, both on their own and as fine points of contrast to more developed work such as the psychedelic wood carvings of the Dayak (which would make for fine-looking tribal tattoos). Items of note were too many to list, but some that stood out of course were the carved penis cover and the decorative artificial vagina, complete with parrot beak (what the...?). Gigantic split drum, overmodeled skulls, Maori artwork, so much more. It all made me want to test the museum's security measures. Just a little bit. Also took in the African art gallery, and the "To Dye For" special exhibit, a display of multicolored textiles upon which different application techniques had been used to create various designs and effects. Of note was a fine Chinese felt rug, the center of which contained a pair of ornamental bats in a circle, the whole being surrounded by an interlocking swastika border.

Then we all went over to the Legion of Honor, big fancy palatial museum (with Rodin's *The Thinker* out front) to see the "special exhibit" "Dutch and Flemish masterworks" and while I'm generally not a big fan of the old masters and what might be considered traditional realism (at this point), some of the stuff was pretty incredible. Very detailed and very realistic, so much so that, behind glass as they were, at some angles they actually looked three-dimensional. Anyway, after lunch we walked through the exhibit "The Mourners": tomb sculptures from a collection of alabaster figures that were beautifully realistic. Their cloaks were so carefully sculpted it looked like they were literally pouring into their stands. Got home, poured some wine, took a nap.

Dinner time: Eliza's on California, featuring Hunan and Mandarin cuisine. I start to second guess the choice of any restaurant the staff of which my hosts describe as "surly," but the waitresses weren't that mean, they just sported the uniform dyke outfit of white workshirt and blue jeans.

Another day, another morning, after coffee and cigarette, went down to Aquatic Park with Dad, squirmed into a wetsuit (with bootie-like wetsuit "socks" and a head covering, plus earplugs), and waded, then dove into the Bay. I had been alternately looking forward to and dreading this; I'd understood that the water was very cold and I envisioned something like instant hypothermia. But it really wasn't that bad, even my face and hands, exposed, didn't numb up too badly. We swam out to the buoy, then along the line of them for a ways. I can't remember when I last went swimming, and not only am I out of shape in the worst (well, not the worst—I could be fat) of ways, but swimming is definitely not a smoker's sport. But I liked it enough (practiced a number of strokes I learned as a kid, and managed not to sink or drown) so even after Dad asked if I wanted to get out and I said okay, we were up the beach at our sandals and hand towels when I said, "as long as we're here, why don't we go another round?" And we did. Granted, both were very short, but it was good. I particularly enjoyed lying on my back and, well, just lying there, floating, looking up into the overcast sky. We got out and conquered the challenge of changing out of wet speedos and into clean dry underwear in a busy parking lot without getting arrested. And then it was over to the Buena Vista for their famous Irish coffee (which was really pretty fucking good) and some classic eggs benedict.

Got up feeling a little lousy (thank you subconscious mind), and wanted a drink right away, but held off and went down to work the upper body on the TRX instead. Then it was a hike down twenty blocks, through the tenderloin, to the Asian Art Museum for the "Bali: Art, Ritual, Performance" exhibit. It was "free first Sunday" which means general entry was free, and only $5 for the special exhibit (sponsored by Target, of all places) as compared to $12 +$5 on any other day. I timed it just right, getting there five minutes after they opened at 10:00... and almost turned around and left. The line was already out the door, down the stairs, and out to the corner. People love free shit. But, I went ahead and got in line, and actually made it inside pretty quickly. Good show, too—loads of masks, carvings and tapestries, puppets, videos of cremation rituals and shadow puppet plays. Very cool. Took some notes, made some sketches. Took a load off for a brief break with some Thai iced tea, then went on to check out the other two floors of the museum's collection. Really beautiful work, especially the netsuke and the incredibly intricate carvings in rare stone. Beautiful statuary as well. Made my offering of 23¢ to Ganesha and took a few pictures with the flash, which I wasn't supposed to but it's not likely to fade the stones. Spent about three hours there. Hit the gift shop on the way out, but after having been there so long already I didn't feel like looking around much more and even their sale stuff seemed expensive. Trudged back home, had a snack, a couple beers, and a nap. Sat outside and smoked, watching jets do maneuvers over the city, sometimes four at a time.

A rather decent day. Dad and Linda got back in town Saturday night, they having spent the week away and I having spent the week mostly curled up in bed with the cats, reading, drinking, and trying not to worry too much about the future. Got rather low at times, but today spoke with Dad about returning to Long Beach, and he said Wednesday would be fine. Briefly outlined my plans for finances and health; he again expressed how much he and Linda had enjoyed the stay, and said he'd be more than willing to help if I needed anything in the future. We watched *The Maltese Falcon* and after a simple lunch we went down to the Kabuki Sundance to see *Contagion*, a film that seemed a lot longer that its nearly two-hour running time, we both agreed. A good time though, the talk and jokes on the walk there and back. Linda made lasagna and after some TV, bed in the very warm night.

The flight from SFO to LAX was remarkably uneventful, and at fifty-one minutes also remarkably brief. In fact, the boarding/unloading of passengers and the taxiing around the runways at either end of the journey took longer than the actual flight.

Checked my bank accounts online: I've got $1,600 left, $400 or more in new bills in the mail. I'm fucked.

San Francisco: a fine place to visit, but I wouldn't want to live there. Again.

Winter, 2011

First full day back in L.B. after two largely excellent months in San Francisco. Got up at 6:00 after a largely sleepless night (woke up around midnight after one-and-a-half hours of sleep; lack of hard alcohol due to the weaning off plan, beer only now back in L.B., for a week, then try to quit entirely, moving towards perhaps quitting smoking after that). Went to Long Beach diner for breakfast, where I was able to eat very little. Went to the bank and transferred the rest of my savings into checking and dumped $400 in cash (big chunk of the earthquake kit money) as well. Went to the PO Box: shit-ton of porno catalogs, the awesome-looking book version of _Esoterra_ that contains an illustration of mine that was used for a cover of the magazine oh-so-long ago, and a bunch of other stuff, some of which remains unopened.

Got up a little late (7:00 AM) after a very sound night's sleep, a little woozy, but coffee and Gatorade helped. Finished the pencils for the PLA design. Started and finished the pencils for a new design I'm planning on sending to Dad. It's based on the trilobite Acidaspis (!) but I'm giving it a more occult/"old ones" look. Grabbed a needed shower, called Celia who's been

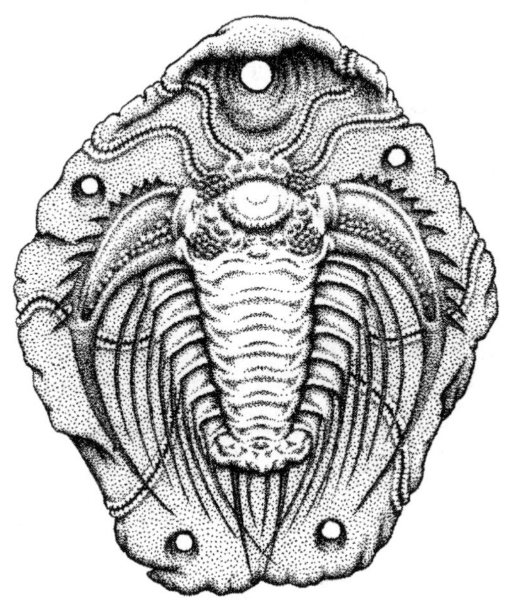

home "sicky" for the past couple days, and we hit Pizza Pi for a pitcher of strong Humboldt Brown, mozzarella sticks, and a big medium "the works" pi. We both agreed it was a fine way to spend the middle of the day in sunny southern California. Watched *Land of the Dead* again with a beer and a cigarette, looking forward to taking a lie down with Welsh's *Crime* and grabbing a nap, looking to relax on my last drinking day (for a while). Joe called: he's in the early stages of excavating the twenty-year hoardings of his estate sale partner Big Gay Dan. Apparently the place is a treasure trove of unique objects, aged garbage, and hordes of various insects. Called Dad and had a good little chat. Called Celia, no response. So kicked it easy and drank the entire twelve of the Pabst I picked up earlier. So, fifteen Pabsts and a half pitcher of beer. Finished the last one just before midnight, and passed out for nine hours.

I am now ahead of "schedule": I had initially intended to quit drinking by Nov. 1 (today), after Halloween, then sober up and start working to take care of business. But I had shortened that timeline by quitting the hard stuff when I got back in town, and then quitting beer after a week. I checked in with the shitty temp agency yesterday, and the timeline for renewing my CA ID, which expired almost two years ago, was "later". Plan for the rest of the day: work on, and hopefully finish, Acidaspis, review and hopefully finish, the "Invade, damage, occupy" essay, work through some more backed-up emails. If I can get the fossil picture done this week, that will be three (minor) pieces completed in one week; more that I've accomplished in months. Exercised, paid some bills. Overwhelmed and depressed briefly; very sad.

Looked over a few hundred job listings this morning. Not much there, either in Long Beach or Pasadena, went by Kinko's, sorted mail, brought some produce at the store. Did some inking, got some exercise. Very tired and sad; almost cried several times for no reason at all. Tried to read Gurosieff's *Beelzebub's Tales to his Grandson*, but it could be a long haul, he's one of those cats who keeps reminding the reader that he's so advanced it's a trial almost to even write about it... and he expects one to read his ten-book series three times... I foresee much skip-page. More inking, computer shit. Worked on the first PLA dispatch—it'll be a double sided one-sheet, folded pamphlet-style into quarters for "delivery"... Really miss publishing, and with no access to free printing and fancy graphics programs, it's back to the old school cheap-ass paste-up. (But I got the paste-up/layout done towards evening, and it does look alright if I do say so myself.) Got to thinking about a case of booze and a carton of cigarettes... passed.

Alright, moving toward getting back on track. Last night went out and bought a couple bottles of Wild Turkey, beer and cigarettes. I know it wasn't a good idea, but 'twas the holiday season god-dang it! Drank my fucking ass off for the first time in months and immediately got reacquainted with the hangover—almost didn't make it to Thanksgiving dinner. Joe was kind enough to come on down and pick me up, and Dayl treated us and a couple rotund cousins of hers from South Carolina to a meal at Din Tai Fung Dumpling House. Went to a bakery in the same strip mall afterward, with an amusing dick arm logo. Got dropped off that evening, don't really remember... spent the next couple days loaded. Got tired of crap TV and headed over to Bliss 525, catty-corner from Vons to see Johnny Mastro and the Mama's Boys play. And they were pretty fuckin' good, even if I don't generally care for Blues. Bill and Celia were there, wasted, with the big Edith Massey—good lookin' lesbian I stepped on a couple times once at Celia's when she passed out on the floor in front of the bathroom. Lots of dances; I reframed. Feeling shitty, so about to get shittier... Mon/Tues down to Pabst, abstaining today, read, napped, and we'll see how it goes...

Brought lotto tickets even after the bonanza of a much needed, much appreciated $5K check from Dad, an "annual dividend from Crites Inc" that went out to all the kids. Double-plus-good. Finished McCarthy's *Suttree* and Jarman's *19 Knives*, both interesting in their own right. At the drawing board, finished the inks for the holiday card. Did some dishes, then to Kinko's in order to shrink the thing down to proper size for the card. Back home to the drawing board to paste up the card and ink the "Senofu Satyr" piece. Plan to photocopy both tomorrow.

Actually got almost seven hours sleep last night, vast improvement over the night before.

Went to Portland to spend Christmas with Dad and Linda. The. Longest. Fucking. Day.

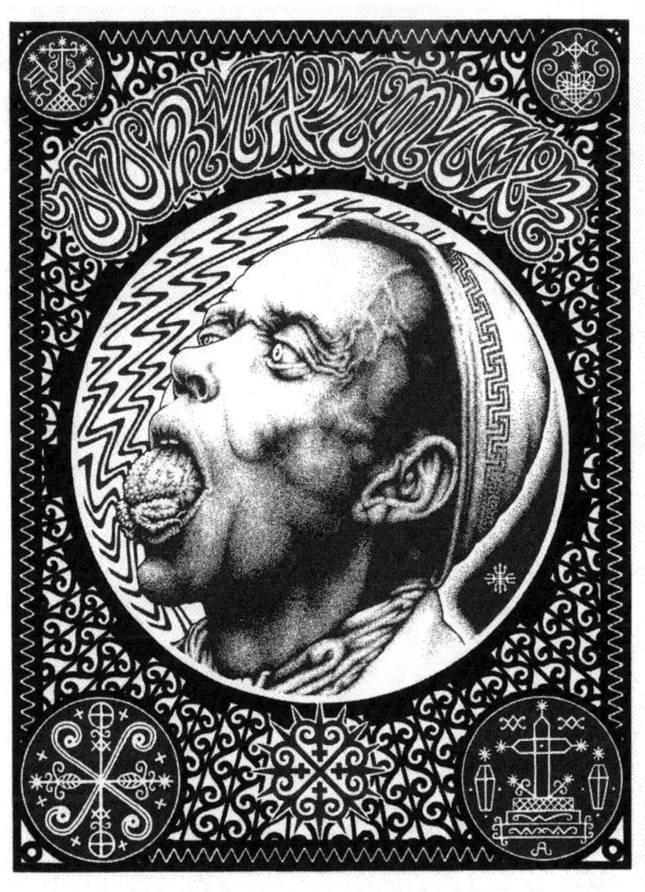

Rehab *Fourth Month*

Friday, November 2, 2012

Long day. Got one brief session of "M" in before dinner (steak, nice), and then graduation "accentuated" by a horde of "dignitaries" arriving for Narconon's twentieth anniversary celebration, which consisted of cutting into the graduation to hold the student body captive as audience to a self-congratulatory executive circle-jerk of this vast parasitic Ponzi scheme in which we are caught. People we don't know, presenting awards to other people we don't know, everyone giving lengthy speeches at every opportunity. It reminds me that it isn't really about the students—it's about the process, the institution. We're just the inmates, at the mercy of the higher powers. Grim. So that whole ordeal went from 6:00 PM 'til 9:00 PM, making me wish I had a box cutter on me.

To Dad fm Tom

Hello—hope all well, if wet, up in the new homeland, and you're still enjoying the change of seasons and scenery. I think we're due for a bit of a rainy period here soon, but the past couple days have been high eighties.

Haven't written in a bit, things being a bit rocky here (nothing nice to say...), but for the moment they're looking up. Just finished the last of "objective exercises," in a nutshell, my opinion remains essentially the same as it was two months ago, but I'm trying to stay afloat and on good terms. (Even if I do generally feel worse than I did when I arrived.)

Reading when I can, just finished The Sparrow, which was definitely a strange one. (Too bad you didn't care for The Gingerman; I haven't read that one in over ten years, may have to try it again.) Margaret sent several books, including The Girl Who Kicked the Hornet's Nest, which I liked very much. Still doing a little bit of sketching, though mostly jotting down ideas to flesh out once I have access to tools, material and facilities.

I did finally get out of the after-dinner chore IC position by filing a five-page "knowledge report" about the problems with that. Now I'm "in charge" of cleaning the course rooms and bathrooms in the morning with my crew of a single crackhead and his running dialog with himself. But, at least I can actually sit down for dinner now. And they did provide a new roommate, Mohammad moved in this weekend.

That's about the size of it, will try to keep you posted as to possible release date. Love to Linda and Rhys,

Love,
Tom

Tuesday, November 6, 2012

This morning got up in good time, got the paper, and breakfast, chore down smooth and easy, even brought the liquid soap around for refills. Got the fresh new notebook and went down to the examiner's office at 10:00 AM, ready for whatever, but my folder was still floating around so I just went back to hang out, which was <u>fine</u>. (Oh yeah: yesterday turned in a form to the health liaison office that Mohammad clued me into, a state disability claim form through which I <u>might</u> be able to receive disability payments for being in rehab and unable to work. Since I haven't drawn a paycheck since 2008 they may reject it, but it's worth a shot...). Did some interview action before lunch, squeezed in a nap after, had some banana cream pie on break: TV reception out, but KUSC had a decent radio show going so read to that. Some of Patricia Cromwell's *The Body Farm* (nice and gruesome). Some of *In Extremis*, even paged through the Bible, finding some good quotes. Had a number of synchronicities today:

1. Aquarius (Jan. 20-Feb.17): The definition of insanity is someone repeating the same mistake with the expectation that things will turn out differently.

2. *Monkey on my Back*, the 1957 B&W flick starring Cameron Mitchell as a championship boxer turned marine corporal turned morphine addict, was on TV around lunch.

3. *King of Queens*, which I never watch but was the only thing coming in, was dealing with therapy in the context of an eating disorder, and in session the big fat guy, when asked how he felt about being there, said "bored and scared, and itchy."

4. And Job 24:17 provided an excellent description of a hangover (in the context of "those who go against the light"): "for the morning is the same to them as the shadow of death."

All in keeping with the theme of addiction, interesting to notice at this time. Got some good ideas down as well: Jotted some additional notes for a portrait of Grann Brijit, including an emblem. Also came up with what would be a great gothic body stocking pattern, a fishnet design spaced with black flowers, fuzzed and tendrilled to mimic decay.

After dinner had to attest to Book 4, write another success story, and have another lengthy interview, with Kelly Anne, which actually went very well. Almost (almost) made me wonder if the negative letter I sent to Dad this morning—the first one in a while... well, had to hedge the bets in case the suicidal depression returns—pave the way in case I have to leave the program. But, for the moment, in the words of Iggy Pop, "I feel alright."

To Tom fm Margaret

Dear Tom

It sounds like you've reached a tilting point with your program and Stockholm syndrome is the next step. I imagine that you can't really actually buy all the stuff they are selling, but in the long run, if it gives you some skills... And you stop trying to off yourself with drinking, you'll be one of their poster children. It does seem that they are being intentionally difficult if they won't actually give you guidance as to why they think you aren't getting it right... You are one of the most intelligent people I know and pretty good at solving the puzzles...

But, bummer to see the light at the end of the tunnel and then realize they've moved the end of the tunnel. I imagine I'd be less than "delightful, damnit" too.

And, yes, it does sound like your roomie was delusional and/or schizoid. There needs to be a fine line between abiding by HIPPA and endangering folks. I suspect that whoever checked him in/is paying for it had tried everything else. Maybe they hoped the scientologists would keep him, put him on one of their ships, and they would be able to stop worrying. I guess he outsmarted them!

Love you

Friday, November 9, 2012

Now into day three of Book 5, "The ups and downs in life" course. Got 100 percent on my first spot check thru sheet, and "clearing" 100 words/day. Lots of verbatim learning, and many clay models to come. Still wondering how long this will all last—come Monday, November will be almost half over... Tonight was graduation, and I'd been working something up all week, but just before dinner our supervisor reminded us that acceptance speeches should be brief, and "all about the wins".

My experience with Book 4 was not brief, and it was not all about the wins. It was heavy, though helpful, but I had to axe it. Still managed to get in a nod to *The Mr. Bill Show* though, which one person at least actually appreciated.

Still awaiting a package from Joe with checks and <u>boots</u> (the Docs are just not right for the cold wet weather we're having, especially with the increasingly gaping hole in the right big toe area), and Dad's response to my last letter, which was the first in a while but did contain some complaints so he may choose again to kick me while I'm down. But I did feel the need to pave the way in case I should need to leave the program. As a microcosm of the larger outside world, it encapsulates everything I dislike about the world: being someplace I do not want to be, put in situations that I do not want to be in, doing things I do not want to do, in the company of people I don't even want to know. All within a strict schedule and a strict set of rules, with next to no peace, quiet or privacy, and aside from books and sleep, no escape or real recreation. And, with full consciousness, the weight of the responsibilities awaiting me outside hanging heavy. Not to mention the guilt trip of the expense, which has most definitely been made known. But I have come full circle twice now, here, from the optimism and confidence I had fresh out of detox to the crushing depression during sauna, then back up to hope and enthusiasm during Book 3, and back down all the way to suicidal ideation during Book 4. At this point "the program" is not helping: where once the idea of drinking was abhorrent, I am now starting to miss the drunken misery of chasing blackouts. At least there I had music. Hope to be done by Xmas... then what.

Book 4:

Most of you don't know me real well. But as I've been here for some months now you might recognize me as a fairly reasonable, quiet, mild-mannered sort. Most of the time, but man, I almost lost my shit on this one. I almost blew the program, and it wouldn't have been a dignified cinematic exit, the long walk down the lonely country road with my thumb out and the Bruce Banner theme playing in the background—it would have been a mess.

But I didn't. One of the things Objectives reminds you is that you are in control of your situation and your environment. I could leave at any time, but as I'd already mastered the epic fail, more times than I care to count, I decided I'd rather go out on/with a win than a quit this time. And I'm glad I did. Objectives also reminded me that there is a lot to appreciate in any situation, and many experiences to be had. These are the things I'd taken for granted, or forgotten, or simply blanked out when I was busy (deliberately) trying to drink myself to death.

Saturday, November 10, 2012

> slept in, still got the paper
> no shitty news in mail
> store order came through—tobacco and Old Spice
> singled out for praise as model student by supe
> got ideas for Cthuchu-style story
> realized coffee a part of attitude problem—calm tea remedy
> close to finishing Book 5

To Tom fm Dad

Hi Tom,

Good to hear from you again. All pretty much the same here. Quite a bit colder than San Francisco and I'm surprised at how early it gets dark.

Lots of large maple trees in the woods here so lots of leaves to rake. And not the fluffy kind we had in Albuquerque—all wet and soggy.

Sorry to hear you "generally feel worse than I did when I arrived" as you could hardly BE worse than when you arrived. If I recall, you were pretty much incoherent and nearly dead. Your crackhead co-worker probably looks the picture of health compared to your entry to the program. You're a smart guy, crackhead was probably the hope and inspiration of some proud parent at some time,—what can you do to get him back on track if the program itself isn't all that helpful?

Enclosed some correspondence re your credit rating. You will be pleased to know you have about the same rating as I do. Can't say I think much of that system.

Take care.

Love,
Dad

Tuesday, November 13, 2012

A little after 2:00 PM, and a good day so far. Just got back from the Ethics office, where I was convinced/encouraged to write to my brother Chris, the first contact in something like eight years. And I actually feel pretty good about it—fairly diplomatic and cheery, without any of the "I'm in rehab and they're making me contact you" overtones. Called Dad for the address, and we had a good chat, which was nice as I was wondering if he'd be reactive about the last letter of mine which was not entirely optimistic or enthusiastic about my current situation. But he was happy to hear from me and thought the letter was a good gesture. I do as well; like I said to him, Chris can write "fuck you" on it and mail it back, sit on it, or write. During lunch I got my IQ and Aptitude scores back, and they are rather encouraging:

	IQ	Aptitude
After withdrawal:	134	71.70
After sauna:	135	83.5
After Objectives:	<u>145</u>	<u>88.41</u>
Out of a possible total of:	155	100.0

Sam from personnel, came through the dining area and we had a pretty good talk—told him I'd finally gotten a chance to play some of the Jesus Lizard CD he burned for me and gave him the <u>Paniscus</u> website address. He seems a pretty cool and interesting cat. I'm playing the disc even now, on a player being tested after repairs by Mohammad, as I have that rarest of commodities, free time, while the case supervisor reviews my file. Mohammad sported me a pack of Marlburo 100s yesterday morning, I still have tobacco and rolling papers from Saturday's Target delivery, snack and mail are up in less than ten minutes, so a brief moment of satisfaction.

Wednesday, November 14, 2012

This place has long ceased to be beneficial in any way. There were two periods since my institutionalization in July where I actually felt good, healthy, confident and optimistic: the first was when I left detox after ten days. This feeling began to ebb almost immediately as I was transferred to the withdrawal cabin, where I was held for about three days and two nights without receiving any accurate information about how long I would be kept there or even why I was being held there. By the time I got down to the main "campus" and was pushed through a lengthy period of "training routines," I was considerably less enthusiastic with the oppressive conditions and regulations, and two weeks into the thirty-one-day sauna regimen my suicidal depression had returned in full.

Once I left sauna and was working my way successfully

through Book Three of the course, I was able to feel that I was making progress, actually learning something applicable, and I was again enthusiastic. During the six-week duration of Book Four this again completely disappeared. The length of the course, and the fact that a significant portion of it, the "objective exercises," were extended and deliberately delayed for no reason for which I was allowed an explanation, reduced my morale completely.

By November I fully wanted to drink again. I found myself thinking regularly that I would rather be half-dead on my bathroom floor. At least there I could be left alone.

Now the second portion of Book Six, the writing up of "overt withholds," violations of moral and ethical codes committed over the years, is in progress. And based upon previous episodes here, this promises to be dragged on for some time as well, possibly weeks, as the program and its staff seek to drag as many confessions of misdeeds from the student as possible: you are not finished until they decide you are finished. From my observations of students working through Books Seven and Eight, the process for those will be the same. The "student" being pushed and prodded and tested and manipulated to staff satisfaction.

I have now passed the point where it was estimated that my completion of the program might occur (mid-November), despite following the program to the letter every step of the way. Although I <u>should</u> finish in December, this is not assured. Thus my confinement is indefinite, and this, on top of the grim daily life at the institution, is more frustrating and depressing than anything else.

My sleep has been affected, my depression has deepened, I have feelings of homicidal rage, and most mornings, even if I do sleep through the night, I wake up in a foul mood. I find myself sometimes skipping meals just so I can lie down in peace for forty minutes or so. Or at least try to.

The utter lack of peace and quiet and privacy has become

wearisome as well. This is not a weekend retreat, a ten-day or even month-long "treatment": I have now been away for over four months, and am considerably the worse for it. You might think a revolving population of junkies, ex-cons, sociopaths and the mentally ill might be interesting, even amusing or inspiring in its way, but it is not. It's like being confined to a high school for the developmentally disabled—that you aren't allowed to leave. And the sole credentials of the school's staff are that they themselves went through the same program.

Which in itself points to something which was strongly indicated from the beginning: the emphasis here at Narconon is not the success of the student, but the success of the Narconon Program. Students who properly "get with the program" are selected and groomed for future staff positions themselves, as were the staff members before them, who are adults not able to function on their own in the outside world: people who have not been rehabilitated for re-entry into society, but for a career in rehabilitation—parasites attached to the underbelly of a larger parasite, a Ponzi scheme masquerading as a rehabilitation program. The only training received being through the Narconon program itself (as evidenced by the on-site staff training programs and the complete absence of certificates from any other institution in staff offices), which itself compensates its members.

Thursday, November 22, 2012—Thanksgiving

Of course there was the white glove cleaning of the course rooms to prepare for the thanksgiving "festivities" tomorrow— which staff also put a wrench into for a number of students by announcing at Monday night muster that all LOAs were being canceled—that's the leave of absence policy that allows students to file for limited day trips off campus with family. So, all of those people who made travel plans previously to fly or drive to Oakview to take their loved ones out to a real meal for the holiday, rather than jockeying for one of eight seats in the dining room, are shit out of luck. Not surprising.

Oh, and the twenty-first marked four months of sobriety.

So today, got up a bit late and found no paper waiting—don't know if Mexicans (ie the delivery lady) celebrate turkey day, or if crackhead Twitch got up early and took it thinking it was his, even though his "subscription" service has been interrupted at least twice for non-payment and he hasn't received a paper all week. Called Joe to say happy thanksgiving, left a message. No breakfast today, "brunch" at 10:00, but I skipped it anyway, settling for yogurt and leftover fruit and the peace and quiet of the room. It was bad enough when Twitch interrupted the morning solace with his humming and muttering and cursing, but now there's a whining bitchy "writer" in there before 7:00 AM as well, and the kids fresh down from the cabin who stayed in bed as long as possible and then crowd the serving/dining area as soon as food is laid out. Yes, every single thing gets a little bit worse every single day.

9:25—made it to roll call, the time of which was still uncertain as of last night; chore moved to 5:30 PM due to the "holiday". Got a piece of bacon to augment the yogurt and "cold pack" of earlier, and even found the paper waiting for me.

Brunch 'til 11:00, then course until 1:30, hors'doevres, and a movie (who knows what, but the options are a ping pong tourney, which I am not qualified for, having played twice in the past fifteen years, or a spades tourney, which I do not know how to play)—or, reading and drawing—still got some ideas to get down.

tom crites

To Tom fm Margaret

Dear Tom:

Happy Thanksgiving.

Thanksgiving was always Granny's favorite holiday. Several years ago, she insisted I stop coming home for thanksgiving because she was afraid I'd be lost if my first holiday not "at home" was after her death. I was still irritable and weepy all day. Her birthday is next Thursday. I've got a day-long meeting out of town. I've already warned my staff I'll be a basket case that day too.

Your last letter sounded less irritated. I imagine you were disappointed to have a release date in mind and then realize it wasn't going to happen. Any thoughts as to when it might? Beyond four months sober, do you feel like you've learned anything helpful?

I am still feeling like I want to head to Portland sometime in the next few months. It is food mecca. Any chance we could coordinate showing up at the same time? How do you feel about spending our birthday together in Portland? We could make Dad take us to swank restaurants.

To Dad fm Tom

Hello—Hope your thanksgiving was a fine one, they did feed us well here.

There is a section of exercises before beginning Book Seven (the second-to-last book of the program) in which we're asked to write down all of the overt acts (transgressions) and their accompanying withholds that we've engaged in across/against the various dynamics (self, family, mankind, etc.). I'm working on the second dynamic, involving family, now, and it did make me think about a number of things. (No, this isn't one of those letters they make you write, but those may come soon.)

I know I have often acted downright ungrateful and thoughtless at times, and I have no excuse for that. I can't really express my appreciation enough for your continued ability, and more than that, your willingness, to assist me through the course of my life and decisions, many of which were questionable, to say the least. From allowing me to move into your home in Gaithersburg (which was not only a <u>much</u> better environment and the happiest year of my life, but which did lead to my meeting Sandra) to helping me move to Long Beach, boots, glasses, teeth, computers... and the schooling that I dropped as well (to which I one day may return, now that I've rekindled and improved my ability to study and learn).

I may have taken and at times did take, these things for granted. It's not that I feel I deserve anything, but I spend so much time alone that I am very self-absorbed, and that makes me very selfish in a way. It's always been difficult for me to really relate to other people in a meaningful way. And while I can get along with almost anyone, I generally prefer to be alone. I haven't ever really fit in entirely, and while I've tried to make the best of it in productive ways, as the return address on this envelope indicates, I have not been entirely successful. This may be part of the reason that I find this situation difficult. So, I do bitch about things here, but at the same time I am actually working very hard to abide by the conditions, and learn as much and get as much out of it as I can.

That being said, there may yet be more griping ahead before the full course has been run... I'm hoping for second or third week of December, but the way they pull things on you here it's hard to tell. Will try to keep good news posted.

Thank you for Christopher's address, I haven't sent this out yet, but will see what happens (after I do mail it, I mean).

Hope all else is well, love to Linda and the girls, and,

Love,
Tom

P.S. Haven't been able to get ahold of Joe lately, so hope all well in that regard and that the mail is flowing as usual. I think the PO Box rental is due this month, which I've mentioned a couple times to him and left petty cash for, so I hope that got taken care of as well.

Friday, November 30, 2012

At any rate, this morning I went to roll call, and was told by the supe that my folder was still out, so I could "hang out"; which means back to the room for peace and quiet. On the way out I gave Marcus the sports pages from the past couple days, and got the windfall of two packs of Fortunas from him as he's quitting smoking again. Been raining smokes lately, got a full pack of Marlboro menthol 100, from Diane earlier for the little pair of nail clippers I couldn't ever use. Then went back to the room and watched a couple episodes of season six of *The Sopranos* on the DVD player Stuart loaned me from next door. (Which was really nice; cold rainy day, all I wanted to do was stay inside and watch movies! Even had buffalo ranch popcorn!) Had some lunch, and once back in the course room I got the good news that the C.S. just had nine of the 162 O/ Ws for me to re-do—and four of those were just too broad to re-work. So, banged those out, got the C.S. pass, and attested with time to start Book Seven, "The ups and downs in life" course. Still have an interview for... something tomorrow morning, but, a full day tomorrow, most of Sunday, and a big start on the week. Schedule says 12/14 graduating, 12/21 might even be OK Steak for dinner, nice! Then graduation, got my Book Six Cert., gave my little speech, and back to the room for some of this and some more *Sopranos*. Went up for a yogurt and tea, got ahold of Joe and had a good chat, received the confirmation that the PO Box rental has been paid up, so good time. Things sound all right, for the nonce.

Prehab 2012

Winter, 2012

A day of misery, but also small triumphs. Quit drinking and smoking again, so it was a long night of vomiting and no sleep, highlighted by depression and anxiety. Vomiting continued through early afternoon, with the attendant shaking, chills, and what felt like heart murmurs. On the positive side, Danny Kerekes from Headpress contacted me and expressed interest in publishing a collection of *Paniscus Revue* reviews. Don't know why, and he admitted up front the "pay is lousy". But if the book does come out, well, it'll be a book. Already transferred loads of files to CD to send (and back up the new PC). So that boosted the spirits a bit. Enough to get me to shave and shower, which had been put off far too long. Even fixed the hot water handle when it came off in my hand! (I think... we'll see how it performs in the long run.) And that fucking car alarm/battery that had been chirping for hours finally got shut off. Huzzah!

Still experiencing some manic mindset in the day, moving into more or less severe depression in the evening, anxiety throughout. Lack of sleep may be a factor, then again with a (more or less) clear mind I have more opportunity to over evaluate everything, think up new ways to think of the worst possible outcome to everything, and dwell on my many past mistakes. Think I may have been misbehaving on Xmas, family fears, etc., etc., etc. Definitely gonna be a Nyquil night, because I need a good night.

Got an email from Herdoktor, he agreed to the $150 for the "Eaten" piece! But he wants to send it to my bank account, so by the bank to confirm as to how to receive a wire transfer from overseas. Finished Dos Passos' *Three Soldiers*. Brought a shower curtain for Celia, as she reminded me a while ago that I ripped hers down one night when drunk (of course I didn't remember; must have fallen ass-backwards into the tub). Liner too. Got gussied up and ready to go see Lisa Cee at Bliss 525. Stopped by Celia's to drop off the shower curtain and liner and a couple coasters from McMenamins, saw Tona and Bobby there, then headed over to the club... Sat at the bar and had a coke, and it was a good set, but I felt really, really sober and really, really out of place. Shot the shit with Johnny when he came in, said goodbye to Lisa and got the fuck out. Maybe should have stayed for the full set, to be more polite, but I just would have been more out of place. Dressing up and showing up was enough I think.

Slept between eight to nine hours! Finally back on schedule. Started prepping and cooking, a process which lasted hours; udon noodles in homemade stock with galangal and sambal and sliced smoked pork hock, reduced it down a bit and it's just about right. Only problem is, the whole vat of ingredients didn't really amount to much. About three bowls' worth, including noodles. Started and finished a propaganda poster piece, "who's watching you?" with tower of London figure/face I'd been wanting to use for a while. Just need to add some op-art expanding circles and ink it, which I can probably do tomorrow.

Celia called to see if I wanted to come over and drink vodka, was pleasantly pissed to discover I was on the wagon again. For dinner took some leftover green tea rice, mixed it with some of the chicken I'd pulled from the stock, which absorbed the flavors very well, and rolled it in bok choy leaves with bastard relish (what I dubbed the mix of chilies, green onion, garlic, basil, lime juice and sesame oil) and ate very well.

I don't know at all what day it is. Been fucking up and fucking around, vomiting, not looking forward to days of anxiety and withdrawal. Fuck me. Fuck my life. Still have to pay bills; need to get washed, need to get shaved, need to do laundry, need to wash dishes, need to find a good method of suicide.

Went through the mail a bit. Got nice cards from Dad and Linda both (with a $150 check from Dad to boot). Had not been looking forward to the internet, but sucked it up and logged on... got confirmation from Georges in Belgium that he'd received the picture and was happy with it, which I was glad to hear. Heard from Kerekes in England and he's still working on book ideas, also good. Got email wishes from all the girls, and Dad, all nice. Tried to catch up on the emails that had amassed since I last logged on, but the security updates slowed that down. Did some reading and Sudoku. Even started the laborious process of cleaning up (but only slightly, only slightly): did some dishes, scrubbed out the toilet bowl (it had reached the critical "kelpie" stage). So, not very festive as far as birthdays go, but not a total wash. Oh, and although I went to bed before 10:30, I was reading *The Monkey Wrench Gang* and all the talk of cowboy cooking made me so hungry I got up at midnight and had part of a bowl of refried beans with chorizo and salsa verde with crackers and club soda (only snacked all day—still testing the belly). And then, of course, I had the shits. Golly, my life is so exciting...

Went online and had a more depressing experience than usual; Laura posted some photos from her garden, and it makes it look like she has a very nice life—she seems much better off with the guy she chose after Paul than she ever would have with me, which is true about pretty much every woman I've met. Which is so fucking depressing I could almost cry.

Beautiful walk on the rounds of errands this morning: it was early, 6:00 A.M., but the sky was already turning blue and the clouds standing out against it were beginning to pick up color of their own. Picked up a paper, figured as long as I was heading downtown to pick up cash anyway I'd check the PO Box again. Scored a package from Robin Bugbee [Bougie] that contained the new issue of *Cinema Sewer* and five copies of the new *Sleazy Slice* with a four-page "Tom Crites Gallery" inside! Score!

On a whim I took the promenade over to Ocean instead of going down Long Beach Blvd and it really made me wish I'd brought my camera: looking past the palm trees to the red lighted clock tower standing up against the burgeoning dawn; the blue lighted pillars lining the promenade walkway; the metal trees by the lamps outside the Renaissance... I may have to go out again later this week and just hope the clouds are as good. Anyway, got cash to tide me over and came on home. And I think the simple therapeutic action of writing in this simple book about my simple life helps as well, reveling in my own douchebaggery.

Got a couple hours sleep, but up around... 4:00 A.M.? Did some drawing, coming close to finishing the pencils on DSD. Designing a black metal-style logo for Whore Church ("Merchants of Awful") and Karen's tattoo. Hit the grocery store early, and when I was unpacking, the tote bag fell off the kitchen table, shattering the big bottle of Superior Light Soy sauce I'd just bought. Soy sauce and broken glass all over the floor. Great tote bag full of soy sauce and broken glass—total write-off. Sunday paper soaked. Groceries soaked. Drag. Cleaned up, had a nice big breakfast of leftover catfish stir-fry, kimchi, "tropical tango" fruit medley and tea. Back to the drawing board. Did that for a while, then made dinner: crawdads boiled in a bit of creole seasoning on top of country greens (collard, turnip, mustard) with peppers, onion and smoked bacon trimmings; fried garlic chips (fried in extra virgin olive oil); and sliced lemon and pepper for garnish. Didn't have alcohol with the meal, but I felt drunk when I finished. Now to sit back and digest, look at the papers and late night comic re-runs.

Spring, 2012

Managed only three hours sleep. Woke up woozy and not in the best of spirits. (At least I didn't have the bad dream of last night.) Anyway, I'd been thinking of methods of suicide lately in the face of my lack of prospects and dwindling resources, and after contemplating sitting in the bathtub with the live end of a severed extension card, think that a bottle of OTC sleeping pills and a liter of liquor. It was only 4:31 A.M. when I recited, out loud, what has become my daily mantra: "I wish I was dead."

But I fortified myself with a cup of double-strong tea and my first cigarette in days, and prepared for the morning errands and what I hope will be a moderately productive day...

Mood improved considerably as the day moved on. Did some Sudoku, cleared the old food out of the fridge and took out the trash. After a couple hours of finishing touches, the DSD piece was finished, and I immediately humped down to Kinko's to photocopy it. Came back posted a couple things. Was in manic mode, very upbeat... for a while. Then depression kicked in a serious way. Spent the many hours of the day and into the night with horrible self-doubt, feelings of misery and worthlessness, bad memories. Even wrote the first draft of my suicide note. Drank countless cups of relaxation teas and smoked endless cigarettes. Finally got to blessed sleep.

Called and talked to Dad and Linda. They're preparing to move to Portland, OR, on or about 4/1 (furniture to follow 4/15, about the same time they leave for S. Africa for a triathlon, returning 5/7). Busy shit. Pretty good talk, which was good as I'd had a feeling that there was a bit of a grudge about the holiday drinking. But everything seems okay.

Withdrawal time again. Shakes, dry heaves, what feels like heart murmurs, shortness of breath despite switching to ultra-light Camel Crush. Vomiting yesterday, gagging today, farting out green slime like a baby. Did manage to get out, copy and mail the rent check. And Celia had broken the window the night before, drunk and locked out, and Bill with her spare key, drunk and otherwise unavailable, so, I took her a tape measure and a piece of poster board to put over the giant hole where the kitchen window used to be. Went out to lunch with the flight attendant next door, Jennie (Reiss?), had a pizza slice or two and a beer each at Pizza Pi. A somewhat interesting lady—used to be a detective sergeant before she got her skull cracked by a meth head. Took her dog Lovely some treats a few days after that, from that special doggie treats store on Broadway. Heard some drilling over next door, peered over the railing and saw

Celia and Tona putting up a piece of board over the broken window. Went out to help, holding the board in place while Tona drilled it in. Provided some duct tape, picked up some of the broken glass.

Actually slept through the night! Woke up a couple times, tossed and turned a little, and have vague recollections of some unsettling dreams, but woke up at 5:45 AM feeling well rested. Got dressed, made the rounds (empty PO Box, get papers, Vons). Home. Ate some fruit medley, washed some dishes, had a bowl of granola, banana and milk, guzzled some orange OJ, pounded some vitamins, got a cup of chai and sugar on the side right now.

At Vons, on top of a painkiller/nighttime sleep aid for the suicide kit, picked up a natural sleep aid that, in conjunction with the Kava and other sleep time teas I hope to pick up at Whole Foods today, should make sleep a dream. Energy level: good, outlook: good. Plan today: day trip down to Whole Foods on PCH to pick up the aforementioned teas and some candy/ toothpicks/misc. munchies to serve as cigarette substitutes. Do some review writing, maybe some sketching, perhaps a nap, some reading, Sudoku, maybe fuck with the PC some more, all remains to be seen. But, I think I've figured out how to both work around to asking Dad for a loan and simultaneously milk my credit to increase my cash flow (while digging a deeper debt hole...). And, to top it all off, I just took a shit so perfectly it didn't even dirty a single sheet of toilet paper. Hell, I'm feeling so good that even if the absolute paranoid pessimistic fantasy of Bugbee and Randall showing up on my doorstep to bitch and punch me out, it would not bother me. Now, brimming with optimism and positive energy, I'll probably get hit by a bus while on my way to purchase herbal tea; that would be great!

Jenny stopped by: "you've got to take a look at what's going on in my apartment." There was yet another leak in the ceiling, this time in the bedroom, and the Mexican contractors the half-shit property management company sent over had cut away a large slice of the ceiling, pulled out loads of (asbestos?) insulation, and exposed old leaky pipes, black rot and mold, all dripping right down onto the heating element wires! And there was talk of asbestos and lead paint dust, and more evidence that "Ocean Realty Advisors" don't really give a rat's ass about the tenants or their health. I got my camera and took a number of pictures, of the hole, the bad pipes, the mold, the discarded insulation, etc., downloaded those onto my PC and transferred them to a flash drive so Jenny could transfer them to her PC in case the whole thing has to go to court and then she vacated the building until it's all taken care of. Doing that photo stuff it looked like the PC was actually going to work for a few minutes, so I went online for a bit, checked and deleted email, touched bases, posted a bit. Hope to type some reviews later, maybe even update the Pansicus Review site... It's now past 11:30 PM and I'm still a bit amped. Am drinking a mix of relaxation/ bedtime teas, but don't want to take sleeping pills/allergy medication unless I need it—expensive and habit making. So, a little late nite TV. Busy, busy day for an unemployed cunt.

Summer, 2012

Misery upon misery here. Took a drunken header down the stairs the other night, and then banged myself up some more once I got home. Now have divots in my head and burses/ scabs on all appendages. So much in pain that I called off the visit to Portland to see Dad and Linda and Rhys (that they'd already paid for...). Thought I'd cracked my upper right arm as the pain was pretty good but it wasn't bruising like it should, and that's subsided now. Tongue swollen and oddly discolored on one side; think I bit it. Hope it was me, and not that rat I killed—a day or so after the anti-climb (which left a pillow case stained with bloody vomit and the sheet and wall splattered). I was sitting on the toilet and, maybe I was hallucinating, but his little fucker walks right out from behind the bathroom door and burrows right into the towel I'd been using as a bathmat. <u>What the shit?!?</u> Didn't know what to do, so got up, got the Fijian war club, and pounded the fucking thing until it moved no more. Wearing the leather work gloves, wrapped it up in the towel, put all that in the trash bag, and threw it the fuck out. Have not seen another one yet, but... Jenny did say she thought there were "roof rats" in the ivy along the fence... Haven't found any holes yet, so here's hoping... and not a shit of a lot else. Bills keep adding up, funds keep running down, glad I... what? I did give Dad a heads up re: fact that I may be begging for a loan soon, but that will only prolong the misery. Have been stocking up on painkillers and sleeping pills. Wait—just found an empty bottle of sleeping pills in the trash; what? Is that why I was so out of it this week that I didn't know what day it was, much less what month?

Rehab *Fifth Month*

Tuesday, December 4, 2012

Woke up in the shittiest of moods—pissed at near everything. Even a decent breakfast, a solid shit, and the first hot shower in days didn't improve my mood. May have been a hangover from the past couple days; yesterday spent almost five hours on a single clay demo ("the formula for the condition of doubt"). And the weekly Hubbard youth rally not only had the now-standard acoustic hamalong singalong (for some...) but the new policy came down that an extra step has now been added to our chore, actually replacing the paper towel rolls in the dispensers in the shitters. Which usually requires a key, but the new cat on the job is not only better and more willing to work than the previous six guys I've worked with, but showed me how to bypass the key requirement for that this morning.

Power did come on after 3:30 PM yesterday, after having been out since 11:30 AM Sunday (Re: power outage: no heat in rooms or hot water, no emergency lights outside, extension cords across the dark walks... and the chores in rainy December conditions...), and my shoes, my single, hole-y pair of Docs, are finally dry (the hour-long chore in the rain and wind that caused the power outage not helping at all). Went to sleep at 8:30 PM Sunday, woke up at 10:30, then took a sleep pack, went back to sleep until... 7:00 AM? 6:30?

So, today, banged out some more clay demos, the mood improved, got a pink sheet spot check on Book Seven I didn't think I was ready for and aced it, and there was orange chicken with hot chilies, noodles, and egg rolls with M&E soy sauce for dinner. Two short periods to go today—here's hoping all continues on the good slope. Did get a couple of books from Dad in the mail yesterday, Miller's *Tropic of Cancer*, which I'm pretty sure I read years ago, and N.S. Naipaul's *A House for Mr. Biswas*, which I know nothing about. Have not yet heard from him re: the letter I sent inspired by the second dynamic (family) O/

Ws, or from Chris re: "hello..." but as those went out only last Monday that seems about fitting.

To Tom fm Dad

Hi Ya, Thomas,

Sorry I missed your call this morning—out for a run. Currently training for a marathon late February in Tokyo, Japan. Nice arrangement, I schedule the events, Linda pays for the travel.

Glad to hear your stay at Oakview is coming to an end, though the transition back into the world will present a new set of challenges. We would like to come down to your graduation if that's permitted and if it wouldn't be awkward for you. Then perhaps you could come back to Portland to visit for Christmas—we'd love to have you but would understand if you wanted to get on to your own life.

You spoke of being self-absorbed/selfish—a problem I've had all my life—a certain amount is required for self-preservation, but I tend to focus on what I want often without considering others and I'm sure the family and you kids suffered for it. It's a character trait of my father as well.

I have told you in the past that if you wish to return to school I'll be glad to help out as much as I can. You would have to have some goal in mind that you are pretty passionate about to make it worth your effort and time. Good place to meet girls though.

Joe continues to send packets of mail every couple weeks, so I think things are being kept fairly even back in L.B. He has been a real friend to us both.

Take care.

Love,
Dad

To Dad fm Tom

Hello—hope all well up your way, I hear that part of the world got some rather severe weather last week. We had a lot of wind and rain, lost power for about a day and a half, but no serious problems. December 21 is the "Postulate Date" at the moment, the date it looks like I should be "graduating"; still have about a week of "Repairing Past Ethics Conditions" to do, the final Book Eight (two to three days), and some wrap-up, so it might be a close one. It would be great if you and Linda wanted to come down (although "ceremonies" is a little underwhelming), and if I don't get out on that date I wouldn't see much point in waiting around another week through the holidays for a token acceptance, so maybe could leave to see you all in Portland just before Christmas. Should be 12/21 though, although they are always pretty vague about these things here.

Very much looking forward to getting back to the world. Not guessing the job market will be much better, but have many ideas to work out and many books to go through. I think that's the thing that bothers me the most about the time spent trying to drink myself to death, not the part about being a miserable drunken ass, but the fact that I simply don't have anything to show for myself for those periods, other than the mess. Planning on picking up the Adobe Suite (Illustrator, PageMaker, and Photoshop), which I learned fairly well on the job in Seattle and, if I can find some of the manuals as well, can bring myself back up to speed on. Will be of use in my own work, and a more solid mark on the résumé.

Another piece about the place I discovered after being invited, after all of the above, to attend night course for the mandatory book "Narconon Field Representation Training Course," which, in effect, teaches you how to shill for the Program. After $35.5K and five months of training, you'll be happy to know you're qualified to sell Narconon products door-to-door, or bribe people for referrals. Yes, finder's fees or referral fees are not uncommon, and there are always those spare event tickets you can pull out to loosen the tongues, is there no shame? No, there is not.

Will continue to keep you posted, love to Linda and the girls,

Love,
Tom

Friday, December 7, 2012

5:25 PM and a very good day indeed so far. Got up about 5:00 AM to get the laundry in and study for the Book Seven test. Did that. Got my cold pack action in. Eggs benedict and fruit for breakfast. Then some more study, and lining up for roll call was additionally surprised to find that I had been elevated from IC of course room bathrooms to the sole proprietor of the staff bathroom in the morning. Did that, hit class and banged out the last of the clay models (did a drill for "repairing past ethics conditions" last night with the supervisor, Richard, who said, "Can I tell you something? You are just awesome, in so many ways." Said it was the best RPEC drill he'd probably had with a student) and "practical assignments" and had from 11:30–1:00 to study some more, then straight into the test after lunch.

Got that done in just over three hours, and may have my test score back tonight—think I passed, here's hoping that the correction order is brief. Free 'til dinner, steak (!), now catching a little blessed Jesus Lizard action on the borrowed CD/DVD player before graduation—should be short and sweet, one lady graduating, I believe. Then the plan is to slack ass, watch *Sopranos*, read, write letters and generally fuck off until the correction order gets done and I can began the actual RPEL process, which takes about a week I understand: my "postulated," or estimated graduation date, is two weeks from now—would be so nice. Dad and Linda want to come down, then have me visit Portland—might be nice too. Assuming the end of the world doesn't arrive first.

To Margaret fm Tom

Dear Margaret,

Hello! Glad to hear your thanksgiving was a grand one. I still try to make Hoppin' John and collards every New Year's Day—Grandmother taught me that if you eat it on New Year's Day you'll have enough to eat all year, and if you have greens with it you'll have folding money in your pocket all year long. I must remember to make it this year! Not a helluva lot else to report—saw a big-ass banana slug the other day, that was a perk. My thanks for the Veloute Manques, another perk! And for the offer of another care package, but I don't think I'll be here for that much longer! Appreciate the thought though, truly. Birthdays in Portland might be good –I'm never very good at planning ahead however, so can't say anything for sure right now...
Cheers to Bruce, and

Love,
Tom

Sunday, December 9, 2012

Not a terrible day at all. Woke up in a bit of a snit, having caught a bit of the creeping fungoo that's been going around, spread by people coughing openly everywhere and rarely washing their hands. And sitting outside from 6:00—7:00 PM in 50° weather doing the RPECS. At a table with other people, with other people coming up asking for paper, cigarettes, whatever, with staff running around shitting and yelling... And the waiting, for the single Ethics Officer and the single Examiner between each step...

Going out to check for the paper again, Stewart next door hailed me to notice the herd of goats roaming around right in front of the building. Beautiful animals, multicolored, some with collars, chomping away at everything available. Nice, somehow. Got the paper. Got the IC position off of my shoulders this Sunday, with the cold, so somebody else got to be responsible for the group of lazy sullen self-absorbed pricks this time. So, even with six people this weekend it took an hour and was a shitty job.

Went back, finished the bathroom, quick shower, and after a frankly lousy hotdog lunch, Jackie cut my long, unruly, neglected hair out in front of the building. Rather nice, actually, out in the sun, getting a haircut from a young lady, to the sounds of Steve Miller and the Eagles... Compliments on the short 'do. She wouldn't even accept anything for it. A nap after that, Asian food dinner, nap after that, newspaper, letter writing, finished season six of *Sopranos*, have to finish <u>Disciples of Cthulhu</u> here before sleep.

Oh yes—got blindsided yesterday into calling the old man to ask about his "intentions and actions" during my high school years, when I started fucking up. He was generously receptive, had some interesting things to say about our funny-colored family history.

To Tom fm Dad

Hi ya Tom,

Glad to hear they have you working through various issues. I think all of us could benefit from examining the decisions we've made and why we chose those particular paths. Not that we can go back to change them, but they help inform how we might make choices in the future.

Many of the choices you made early in life were made by others and forced on you or were reactions (normal for youth I think) to situations you were in. It's more of interest as how those choices lead to choices you've made later in life, on your own, and how you adapt your background at this point to build a better life. Hopefully people there can help because I don't have a clue how one does that.

I read an article in the paper today about people in their forties going to med school. I think you'd make a fine doctor—like your great grandfather Haw. Actually I think you'll make a great whatever you put your mind to.

Love,
Dad

Saturday, December 15, 2012

Well, 12/12/12 came and went without event, and Thursday, 12/13/2012, was actually a good day: saw the goat herd again, eleven beautiful multicolored animals munching the shit out of the grounds. I <u>think</u> I finished the "repairing past ethics conditions" routine, taught another student, Laura, how to play "the game with no name". Saw a shooting star (as I was meditating the almighty prayer)... and then Friday: found out the "present time conditions" I'd worked on the night before and before 7:00 AM that morning (while doing a load of laundry) all needed to be rewritten in full RPEC format... So did that. The "postulate date": for my graduation has been pushed back from 12/21 to 12/28 (which is a short week itself, Monday being Xmas eve with limited course time, no course time on Xmas), which may mean another week as I'd hoped maybe if I didn't graduate Friday 12/21, I could finish Sat. or Monday and go to Portland for the holiday, but, no. So, re-wrote the PTLs all day yesterday, turned them in just before the fourth period ended. Then graduation, 1:25 hours, four grads—got to listen to the sociopath soapbox again about loving everybody... but he's outta here now.

Later: Did move on to "exchange": with a bit of a wait and the student-wide interviews inspired by a pruno incident,

Tessr, a former student now staff trainee with facial tattoos and piercings, got me through it in three course periods. After finishing and attesting I asked the supe if I could get Book Eight to read and start clearing words, even though it would be Monday before I knew what the next step would be for sure: the answer was no, I'd have to attest first. So, that's a day during the week wasted, and Sunday wasted: that's two days: which is about exactly what it takes to get through Book Eight, which is about exactly the amount of time I would have needed to graduate by 12/21.

To Tom fm Dad

Hi Tom,

So I'm thinking we will pick you up at Oakview, Friday, 12/21, and go back to San Francisco for dinner and the night. At that point, depending on what you want to do, I can put you on a plane for Long Beach, or you can return to Portland to spend a few days with us, then back to Long Beach. Let us know as plane tickets are cheaper seven days in advance and Christmas travel can be a bit hectic.

Thinking back on our recent phone calls (and I think it's a great exercise you're undergoing, though not easy I'm sure) though I don't much question the choices you made in high school, those in years that follow one might question. I assume you'll get to that in some progression, but if not:

leaving the scene of your hit & run accident—bad choice, though understandable with an angry mob piling out of various doors in the middle of the night, it's typical conflict avoidance we both chose and need to meet head on.

Leaving college before graduation—and that close! We made a mistake in not giving you work breaks and force feeding too much academics but a change of major or some redirection like Bill Gates or Steve Jobs might have worked better.

Fran had a job history of deep commitment, hard work, burn out, move on, which leads to a varied resume, but not long-term stability/ success. Perhaps we'll talk about decisions following high school and your life at home and we can cover these points.
Hope you are well—looking forward to seeing you again.

Love,
Dad

Sunday, December 16, 2012

A day of challenges met. Woke up at 3:00 AM, coughing, stress: took a sleep pack, cough drop, cigarette, cup of calm tea around 4:00, got back to sleep around 5:00 AM and slept until 7:00. Breakfast, got a seat among the crowd of new kids. Called Dad, left a message re: delayed postulate date, able to do so in the rare moment when homesick twats not monopolizing phones. Got paper. Read paper. Did the room cleaning, went to the white glove for the courtyard, which I'd been dreading, but worked out okay. Then a hot shower, some drawing. Chicken sliders, fried fish and apple for lunch, nice. Some more drawing, nice undisturbed forty-five-minute nap, mint chocolate chip ice cream for snack, watched some episodes of *Rescue Me*, played cards with Laura, Chinese food for dinner, cards with Laura and Cory, and R&R in the room to myself by 8:00 PM. All right.

To Tom fm Chris

Hello Tom,

tom crites

Thank you for your letter. It was great to hear from you as I have been wondering how you have been doing. Things are going well here. Growing lots of food and had a pretty crazy garden this year. Radishes, peas, beans, quinoa, Chinese broccoli, tomatoes, potatoes, beets, chard, kale, zucchini, spinach, lettuce and stuff. Probably had over ten pounds of tomatoes and over five pounds of potatoes. Been making my own kimchee and sauerkraut, which is easy and delicious.

Keeping busy painting. Still making the mug shots on paper bags. Other things as well, but primarily the mug shots. Started painting them on those big yard waste bags which is intense, as they are almost five feet by almost four feet wide. Glad to hear you are still making art.

Bought a motorcycle a couple years ago and it is unbelievably fun to ride. It's a 1974 Yamaha 350, so is light and small enough to be manageable. Also old enough to be pretty easy to work on. Riding season is pretty short up here and the clutch went out this summer so I got to figure that out before spring.

Have you seen Dad and Linda's new house in Portland yet? It is pretty incredible.

Take it easy and thanks again.

Chris

To Tom fm Dad

Hi Tom,

A bit of mail, decided not to send the books, neither was very good and there was some question about delivery time with the Christmas rush.

Didn't know you subscribed to the <u>San Francisco Chronicle</u>—may want to cancel that to avoid the credit card charges.

Enclosed your Christmas present. Not much Crites Inc dividend this year, it all went to other purposes. Sorry you have to spend Christmas with strangers, but good to see the course to its full conclusion.

Had a bit of snow here this morning—nothing to stick to the ground, but seasonal.

See you soon.

Love,
Dad

Thursday, December 20, 2012

Thursday... Just took the Book Eight test "The way to happiness"... almost three-and-a-half hours. Don't have any idea how I did. Worked the fucking practices all PM Tuesday and Wednesday. Started Monday—after being held up for an hour-and-a-half for student-wide piss test: some kid ate a bunch of pills and everybody pays for it. This following last week's room search because some other asshole was trying to make pruno: he got suspended, we don't get orange juice in the morning anymore. Then yesterday Chitler got some order to go around looking for reasons to hand out chits, so everyone in the ghetto got one, including our room, for "not vacuuming": it was done to standard Sunday for white glove, and this room has never received a chit in five months. I picked up knowledge reports for the group, and submitted a stack to Ethics (from mine: "If this would be any attempt to round up manual landscaping labor, I would consider that unethical"). Still got the chit.

On Tuesday talked to Lisa about getting together with her sometime about folks visiting on graduation, still scheduled for Friday the 28th, and she said probably later that afternoon: nothing. So, morale nice and low. What a shithole. But then, after the most uninspiring dinner in recent memory (master chef Hung being off), consisting of bits of frozen chicken breast in flavorless oily sauce, dry flavorless fried potatoes, some kind of flavorless beige beans with a few carrots, and grilled zucchini stuffed with cream cheese and breadcrumbs, I received word that I passed the Book Eight test—100 percent. My average across six tests is now 98.333 percent. Did the course room white glove, getting IC of tables, second easiest only to chairs. And then, a rare bit of free time.

To Tom fm Margaret

Dear Tom:

Cheers on acing book Seven! Nice to have the light coming at you look like the end of the tunnel rather than a train, eh?

Tomorrow, my office is having a holiday drop-in. I don't know about where you are, but where I live is "war on Christmas central." Frankly, I'm surprised I've not caught crap already for calling it a "holiday drop-in" rather than "Christmas." The state was very late in getting funds to us, so we don't have much in the way of furniture or decorations for the new office. Oh well. Maybe this will inspire some donations. I made a fruitcake biscotti... Didn't work out the way the recipe said it would, but tastes okay. I also made oatmeal cookies with mini M&Ms in them. And this afternoon, I'm making a double chocolate peppermint cookie, with crushed candy cane on the tops as decoration. It probably wasn't the smartest timing I've ever done to make two new recipes for an event. Oh well. We're also going to serve hot cider with orange slices and spices in it. The real point is to let people see our new office and meet our newest employee.

So, Granddaddy told Cathy a few weeks ago he was headed to Missouri. Some time went by and she didn't hear from him, so she called someone in Missouri who keeps tabs on Granddaddy. He said Granddaddy hadn't been there. Cathy calls the NC house and he says he didn't go because he got a cold. Now, the last time Cathy talked to him he said he literally was walking out the door to go to Missouri... So I don't understand how he caught a cold between the phone and the door.

But, Cathy has set up a schedule for people to call him every day. My day is Tuesday. He seems chipper. Seems happy to have someone to talk to. His voice is shot. He actually told me it was because Granny caught him with her cane. He downplayed it... Like he didn't want me to think she did it on purpose. He seemed annoyed that I'm not coming home for Christmas... But he told everyone he'd be in Missouri by now. I did send him a load of books, so hopefully those will keep him out of trouble.

We haven't heard from the friends we normally spend New Year's with... So we think we may have a quiet New Year's at home... Fire up the smoker and smoke anything that isn't tied down. I want to throw some tomatoes on the smoker and then make pasta sauce out of the smoked tomatoes.

I hope you get sprung soon. I kinda have to plan in advance when I'm going to be out of the office. I think I'll email Dad and see what he thinks of the idea of having us visit for our birthday. I give you first refusal. I'd love to see you again.

Love you

Sunday, December 23, 2012

So, yesterday I started the "Phase IV" sequence. After an hour and a half interview, still have not been told what "Phase IV" is, but it started with... going all the way back to TR 0, eyes closed. For almost three hours. Like the punishment they give people for fucking around on course; not telling me for how long (I assume) or what's next (I asked) or... if I'll be graduating Friday, 12/28: no definite answer. I told supe Danny, I needed to know, as folks would be traveling down. He checked—no solid answer. I went ahead and told him I was ready to leave Monday if I couldn't get an answer, as the lady who would have an answer was gone for the day. Said he'd do what he could to help me out, but, here I am again, not being told shit, on the ass-end of the train. I've seen them fast-track the kids they were lining up for staff positions, I've seen them do favors for the popular student-of-the-week kids (Sunday Phase IV sessions for the sociopath). Called Dad, but he seemed to think, based on conversations with family liaison earlier (Thursday?) that Friday was a go; he's going to leave Portland on 12/27, by car, show up for dinner, and it's going to be... time to go after that. Probably to Portland. So, I may work my sad, sorry, frustrated ass off until then, and bail.

So, still seething over that, went to bed at 10:00 PM. Got up to piss around midnight, took a sleep pack; got up to piss around 4:00 AM, couldn't get back to sleep. Muhammad got up at 5:30 AM, went out, came back. And a little before 6:00 AM, I hear the belt buckle go... oh no... and the fucking old meth monkey starts jerking it right in the next bed. Couldn't take it—got out of bed with a "God Damn! Are you fucking kidding?!" Put on the coat and shoes and out—into the rain. Asked the desk guy, "Hey, I've got a question: my roommate just creeped me out and disturbed my sleep by jacking off right next to me—what's the procedure for that?" Horrified look.

And a suggestion for a KR. Was trying to compose one in the dining room and, yes, Twitch comes in. With the surprising, and the mumbling, and the singing and talking to himself. Fucking funny farm. Got through breakfast, spent an hour cleaning the bathroom (found shit on the tank up by the handle the other day—I'm fucking speechless), read some of the paper, then, yes, an hour out in the courtyard in the rain, scrubbing, picking up cigarette butts, etc. My shoes are still wet. I changed socks three times. Got a shave and shower. Tried to get a nap, no dice, of course. Day skulked by. Oh, after sitting on the KR that I did eventually finish, I turned it in—in case some even more disturbing shit goes down. And I did make it a point that I'd known about them knowing about TJ being a schizo, and about them not doing nearly enough about Twitch, so that's all on the record. Ethics talked to me at dinner, got the message, he'll be off to Placerville Wednesday. Not soon enough... Test after test. And that report grows and grows and grows.

Monday, December 24, 2012

Amazing halo around the moon tonight—bright star (Jupiter?) inside. Not a cloudy night, stars visible on either side. Heavenly sign? Sign of imminent apocalypse? Beautiful either way.

Friday, December 28, 2012

Busy, busy week. Started the "Phase IV" on the weekend, even working into Xmas eve and Xmas, many thanks to an assigned "twin", a supe and an examiner. Finished on Wed. Then what turned into thirty-page "Admin Scales" work that was to cover goals, purposes, plans, programs, projects, orders, ideal scene, statistics, valuable final projects, etc.—which, along with various interviews, went past 5:00 PM. Dad was waiting in the "lobby" when I finished, and we had a bland meal of ham, potatoes, and rice. Then the graduation ceremony—fairly merciful and brief, when it came time for me to get my plaque I got the standing O, ("thank you, thank you... thank you. Thank you... thank you, thank you!"), did my speech, which I believe came off all right, another stander that continued after I sat, and Dad said a few brief words, then Marcus, Paul, and John got up and said some really complimentary things on my behalf, about being a model and an inspiration, etc. (Nicely following supe Richard's earlier words in the examiner's office about my being a model student.) Did a few handshakes and hugs, finished the packing, got another photo taken (passed the "opportunity" to have my "image or likeness" used as promotional fodder), got my fucking property back ("contraband"—including the topless photo postcard from months ago), and... got the <u>fuck</u> out of there.

The whole way down the long, winding road from the Oakview Center, in the dark, I kept expecting armed guards and WWII barbed wire fencing barriers to spring out. Five fucking months... God damn.

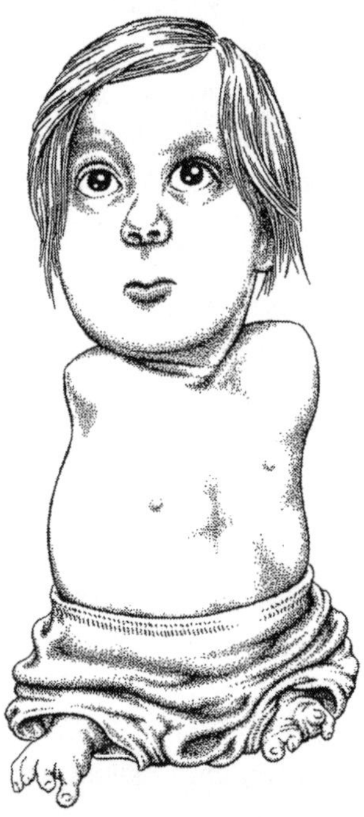

Posthab *2013*

Spring, 2013

Well damn—it's been a long time. Locked away for five months in detox/rehab, then too busy to write here, literally. So, to begin afresh from today, up at 5:30 A.M., coffee and cigarette and the paste-up of *Planarian Liberation Army* Vol. II, No. III (Issue 8). Out to photocopy, back to do some Facebook and start afresh with the job search here in Long Beach with the much longer list of employment agencies found recently online through Bing/Yellow pages. Posting résumés, filling out applications, checking job postings... Some Facebook time, including writing and posting of reviews for the PLA and the movie *John Dies at the End* (on the Paniscus Review Facebook page, established as a foundation for promoting the Headpress book, the contractual agreement for which was received, signed and returned Saturday directly following my return from Fargo). Washed some dishes, did exercises (forty 8 lb curls, vertical pushes, lifts, horizontal presses, twenty lateral lifts, 150 crunches).

Around 1:30 went out with Jonny and Lisa to Siem Reap in Cambodia town for lunch and good friendly conversation. I'd offered to do the posters for them in San Fran style, loaned them a couple catalogs, so that may help spread some word of mouth for future work they'd talked about.

Came home and grabbed an hour's nap after calling my PO, Carrie, at Narconon. Got up, coffee and cigarette and back to the PC for obligatory Facebook and more exploration of the employment options. Graphed out a bit of an idea for a "negative gravitational response" poster, a suicide girl with the car hood she landed on forming a haw/manderla/coffin with psych lettering. That and the Grann Brijit are the next two large pieces; so far this year I've managed to complete three PLAs, the large ganesh 2013 piece (original going to Dad), and the "Phibes Publishing" and "Devil Bunnies local 2s" "logos". Joe and Bonnie came by, got me set up as a seller on Amazon.com to start moving excess media—I'm now the head proprietor of Tom's Media—hooray!

Oh yeah, fringe benefit from lunch, $48.00 in cash from Johnny and Lisa as I put the meal on the heavy credit card balance. Which is good, because I'm down to $800 in checking: gonna have to try to use WF credit to "bill pay" for now, although I hedged my bets by already putting forth the depressing proposition of yet another loan from Dad—which he says will be okay, as long as I'm not drinking.

Got up late, 6:00 A.M., to find another item had been sold on Amazon (*Lustful Addiction* DVD, w/poster) and I'd gotten A+ response from D. Grrr, tattoo artist in Paris and former *Malefact* contributor, re: the upcoming book. Did the job hunt online, looked at I don't know how many fucking job listings, some more inking, sent out more enquires re: art book. Got the iCloud set up on the PC so I can transfer photos from phone and enable the "find my iPhone" feature and almost missed the alley festival outside. The fat retard from the building next door trying to sweep trash into a kitchen dustpan with a push-broom while talking to it, the trash, and the little psycho Marx Brothers-lookin' bum lady who sprawled out on the dumped couch for a while, orating about getting fucked on the champagne roof and her one eye... it was annoying until I started paying attention to it, then brilliant.

So, that was a weekend: metro'd out to Sierra Madre Wednesday afternoon, after confirming w/Ocean Realty that the rent check had actually made it to 'em (it had been received and deposited the previous night—the lady was as kind and helpful as could be, and even asked if anyone had ever told me I should be a radio announcer...!).

Thursday up and out early to the Civic Center in Glendale to hang paper all day (like last year) for the Art and Antiquities show. Sunday out to porter for the show's end, another $85.00 cash for two-and-a-half hours. Not a good show for the dealers: even if not as many sellers as previous years there were still more vendors than buyers so not a lot of money being made. No pity on my part, snobby over-charging under-paying bastards can struggle with their garbage somewhere else. Got a lift home, getting back around 9:30 PM Unwound, unpacked, sacked out. Managed to have a good time for the most part however, and made enough to pay the visa bill this month.

Eight months sober

Up at 5:15 AM to make coffee. Out of sorts, with a knot in the upper back. Don't know where that came from, lifts and crunches were the day before yesterday. Took out the trash, hit the grocery. Got a call from Carrie, she thanked me for the Pappy's Day card and we had a decent chat, she was very encouraging ("you're doing everything you're supposed to do") and glad to hear of the small successes. Did some scanning and put together some new PLA pieces. Some sketching, some more inking on the new drawing "Anemone" which came together over the past couple days, prepared a very decent steak and habanero burrito meal, got rid of some old weeklies that had been on the hat chair for a year. Got a surprise in the mail this afternoon, distribution from "Crites, Inc."—to the tune of $2K. Much needed, and much appreciated. Breathing room! Worked on the art solicitations for the book project (some back and forth) until almost 10:00 PM

My lungs are laboring and I can't smoke enough to ease the constant tension, which nicotine doesn't seem to help, and caffeine just seems to fuel that anxiety. After yesterday's horror route of "everyone's an ignorant ass and I'm one of them" I have to try to quit both; now seems a good time, with a small safety net in the bank and no social or professional demands at the moment, so plan to stay in today, sleep, read, sort through some for-sale potential shit, and cold turkey it.

Fighting depression. More job search, which seems at this point like a purely token effort. The worse will come when I actually land a job and have that hanging around my neck and over my head every single godamn day. Still not seeing the point of it all, still not able to visualize any viable scenario that provides a sustainable level of gratification... Drugs and death on the mind, no excitement or enthusiasm for anything—need sleep...

The flares of stress, anxiety, and depression simply refuse to lift. Tried to engage in black mirror meditation yesterday, and was so wound up was unable to focus or center. Need more discipline there. Also need to focus on the art; try something different? New medium? The quick and random "graphic design" of PLA is good at times, but hardly enough, then again, it's never enough…

Slept a little fitfully until about 6:30 AM. Checked email and online site, looked for jobs (applied for a publications asst./graphic artist position in Goleta yesterday), got a call from Dad, had a nice chat, did the light lifts and the crunches, showered and shaved, had the lunch, and got the urge to get out to the liquor store—to buy a Powerball ticket for the State's first drawing tonight (lottery). Did some penciling on the new project, underground commix, "Jawohl", a kind of lowbrow cross between Shakes and El Topo, the character and storyboards for the first "episode" which I sketched up yesterday. Then lay down to read (Conrad's *The Secret Agent*) and doze a bit. Wasting a bit of time the past couple days playing the iPhone app "Candy Crush". Gotta keep that light. Also yesterday had a decent online chat with Margaret while on FB. Did a little graphic design… Left a message for Carrie.

Summer, 2013

Ten months sober.

Really a nice day. Up at 5:30 AM, hiked to the PO even though I was there Saturday, as the climbing machine finally broke this weekend. After over ten years in my possession, after retrieving it from the giveaway room at the shit building in Seattle (nice apartment, though) the cord finally broke. Really a pretty ideal day: art, reading, recreation, cooking. Did some scanning and design, called the Oakview P.O. and finally got the names of the IQ (Novis) and aptitude (Oxford) tests we'd batteried… I'd been a bit aggravated after seeing a post of Chris' indicating that he'd received some sort of grant from the Artist's Trust of Washington. Being rewarded for color-by-number paintings of other people's work made me feel, for a moment, like I'd failed as an artist. But, kudos for milking the pop art market. Soothed my soul by thinking that in ten years those paintings will be behind some couch in some garage, removed to make room for the next colorful trend. And, finally, that those footsteps in the sands of time and art history won't be any deeper than anybody else's. Still working on present time, and as I think of it, "the brand new minute"; will make the determined effort to keep the positive and productive days coming. Nothing like being left to my own devices.

Tired these days... very tired. Will try coffee again today, after a couple weeks without, but will probably just make me spastic, anxious. Three short sets of meditation today. Planned out five or six pages for PLA 17; had an idea for an "Ocelot Rising" drawing, started two different sketches (based on the Lost Sounds song of the same name), and it was evening before I worked out that I needed to do it full poster size, rather than the quick one-day drawing I'd initially envisioned. Exercised, watched the 2011 version of *The Thing*. And prepared what turned out to be a most excellent meal: baked chicken with Chinese five spices, garlic power, sea salt, cayenne and peppercorn mélange, and green beans stir fried with garlic and ginger plus onion, red jalapeno, peppercorn mélange, and mirin and tamari (in peanut and sesame oil) really, really tasty and satisfying. Called Dad, had a nice chat, then pasted up the PLA until almost 10:00 PM. Did not get to the paper or other studying...

Most of the day occupied with the psykedayakali picture, still filling out Mcory—may be able to finish the pencils tomorrow? Had a great mix on the CD player for part of that, Bauhaus, Apocalypse Theatre, Nocturne, Sex Gang Children and Specimen, and while drawing to that, actually felt an amazing and rare surge of happiness. Must do that again. Back to the job search, that is getting more and more disheartening. I keep adding job search sites, but the number of jobs I'm qualified for seems to keep diminishing. Depression, anger, anxiety all almost omnipresent, what with the bill pay account and the savings account down to $1,500, will have to start looking for caretaker positions—a haunted mansion, a deserted lighthouse ... somewhere where I can be left alone. Don't really think that will happen though, any more than the lottery win will come through. Don't know what to do. Keep walking though.

Working on writing a piece for Johnno's Paranorm site, and he wants a load of illustrations for his video(s) to replace those he's using that he doesn't own the rights to (and can then sell more on e-Bay). After sending multiple treatments of three pieces, each of which took hours to complete, I quoted him $60 apiece for the projected sixty pieces. Says he: I was hoping for single line drawings at $7-$10 apiece. Still negotiating, but he's paid before and is prepared to do so again. Am hoping the

Paranorm thing works out, not only would I not have to look for work every day for the next month, but I could maybe even add it to my résumé. Credit on the bill pay account is almost gone, checking won't cover August... And my Powerball numbers did not come through again—no surprise there. So, typed in and edited the review of *You Will Die*, should be able to post that soon. Called Carrie at Narconon, she acknowledged that this was the last check-in of the six-month period, congratulated me on my sobriety—progress. Okay! Got a response from Johnno on the ballpoint pen sketch of Bigfoot: "Yes! That's perfect... very excited now!" So, I'll bang out fifty shitty ballpoint pen sketches. $500 is a lot less than $3,000, but still more than $0.

Good day so far, for 8:30 AM... Party fags didn't wake me up again as they did last night (if they had I would have considered returning the favor with a 6:30 AM "courtesy call"). I did wake at 2:00 AM, a cigarette, herbal tea and vanilla yogurt got me back down. Up to alarm begrudgingly at 5:30, hit the grocery store and started the stockholding of booze and cigarettes for the breakdown I am anticipating—come the twenty-first it'll be a year of sobriety and of late I haven't been feeling too much better about things. But for now I finished laying out and printing up PLA 19, and scanned the second/background versions of the latest cryptids set. I've got to get on the final stages of the cryptids, and I found the face I think I want to use as the Medusa for the stalled Octopussy tattoo piece. Also have an idea as to how to satisfactorily finalize the banana flower piece. There're papers to read, but I do believe it's animation domination night, with BBQ chicken.

Spent some time working out the design/elements for a psykedayakali piece. Did not look for work, did not meditate. Did some sketching, exercised despite another reoccurrence of severe depression. Wrote a suicide note, did some scanning, some PC shit, then out to Kinko's to copy the latest cryptid completions. Did the lifts and crunches, a brief job search and pulled some images for the next cryptids set. Along the way I had something of a change of ideas regarding plans: next Sunday will mark my one-year anniversary of sobriety, and as it has been otherwise a hard, fruitless, miserable year, I was considering starting drinking heavily again with the sole aim of suicide at the end of savings. Already have the mason jar of cigarette butts (#1), with two bottles of sleeping pills (#2) and the hair dryer in the bathtub (#3), with 1.75 liter bottles of Canadian Club, Bacardi Gold, and Popov vodka (#4). Adjusted the Netflix queue and added three-at-a-time option to my plan so I'll have movies coming in to watch regularly. Will take a week off: eating, drinking, maybe even going out for meals and drinks, starting Sunday and going through the next. Looking forward to ice cream and rum for breakfast.

I still haven't gotten a call back from my call to Dad Thursday evening, which was essentially the touching of base meant to head off the same during my week of vacation which was to start tomorrow—around 3:00 AM or whenever I got up. Got the Amazon account deactivated, current on bills, have seven liters of booze, eighteen beers and seven packs of cigarettes—all I wanted was to sit and drink and watch movies, the only thing I've had to look forward to in a long time, but the paranoid thought hit me that not only may he be waiting to call and "congratulate" me on the anniversary of my sobriety just when I was breaking that, but, even worse, what if he decides to pull a surprise visit/inspection to see how his precious "investment" is doing? Crumb, so, some anxieties there. Can't get wasted on Sunday unless I hear from him. And more than that, had to stash all the hooch and the jar of cigarette butts, and the beer won't be ready when I am in any case. Will have to stay on the wagon until this is resolved. Spoils my selfish plans. Fuck me twice.

So... kind of a useless week. Spent all yesterday recovering, sleepless, vomiting and retching, gagging so much my throat is still sore. So got online, checked email, then took out the trash, picked up Saturday's mail, down to Ocean Blvd for *OC Weekly* (no L.A. weeklies), hit the PO to post bills due the first and second and check the box. Feeling a little tired as I hadn't been out this much or eaten much in days. But I was able to take my first shave and shower in a week yesterday so was cleaner than I'd been in a while. Back online again, looking for jobs and collecting and printing more pictures for the Crytid project.

Woke up feeling shitty, tired and depressed, so drank some tea and worked on the suicide note. Then put together about five PLA packages. Did some dishes, got inspired by the busy work, did a very little bit of reading in *The Hellbound Heart*. Got to thinking it is a matter of taking care of business, should be doing some work during the daytime here, rather than lying around, maybe ought to, for now, treat the little work I've got like a job, try and put closer to eight hours into it. Feeling oddly content—a rare and beautiful thing. Rather more calm and focused lately, perhaps due to the very present thought that this month might be my last.

The End

tom crites

About a year after entering rehab, August 19, 2013, Tom posted the following letter, took two bottles of sleeping pills with a bottle of vodka, and died.

August, 2013

Dear People,

I hope this letter finds you well. I regret to inform you that by the time of its receipt I will have most likely passed away, and am writing in advance for the reasons detailed below with the hope that I will be able to post it in proper time.

It has now been over one full year since I entered rehabilitation for chronic alcoholism (itself only a symptom of a larger lifelong condition), and it has been a year full of frustration, rejection and disappointment. At this time I actually feel worse than I did than when I was physically near death. It is true that I was miserable a year ago, however it was a simple, bleak, animal misery; now with full consciousness I can appreciate the extent of my failures on multiple levels, compounded by increasing debt and despair, and the anxiety and depression this causes gives me no peace. Every waking moment, and even in sleep, I am reminded of my shortcomings, and it has reached the point that every single memory or interaction, no matter how small, reminds me painfully of another link in a seemingly endless chain of inadequacies and frustrations that I am no longer able to bear.

There is no longer anything that I want from life. There is no joy for me now. Every time I feel some small measure of personal success or achievement, something comes along to remove that. Having tried many things in many different arenas and found lasting satisfaction in none of them, I no longer have any goals or desires, and therefore nothing to work toward; nothing to live for. Never-ending obligations, demands, interruptions and pressures, both external and internal, make it impossible to simply be left alone in peace. But even if this were possible, there would be no pleasure in that life: seeing people as generally horrible creatures, I am caught between the positions of not being able to stand being in the company of others yet still having the innate need for social and emotional support. I am unable to make meaningful connections with others, with the world, and I see no viable scenario which would provide the gratification sufficient to make the continuing effort worthwhile. In every professional and social environment in which I have functioned I have not found any lasting fulfillment, and at this late date I anticipate only further frustration in any future efforts. I have been alone for so long now that I no longer have anything to offer to others, or to the world. And they have nothing to offer me.

I am very tired, and crushing depression regarding the nature of my condition makes it impossible to continue. Attempts at self-improvement and moderation, such as exercise, study, meditation, proper diet, dietary supplements, proper sleep, herbal teas, practicing writing and drawing, have not been sufficient. I do not wish to struggle any longer, I simply want it all to stop.

As I have been considering suicide since the age of 12, and having failed at my previous five attempts, I will try again. And again. At this point I have been institutionalized twice, hospitalized multiple times, and seen countless doctors, counselors and 'mental health professionals,' and as none of this has done me any good at all I see no point in pursuing further 'professional help.' And I have absolutely no wish to begin endless trial runs of prescribed medications with countless negative side effects with the sole goal of maintaining a base existence sufficient only to continue to work toward a state of prolonged misery and even slower death.

And so I write this now in a state of mind and body as sound as I am capable of possessing. I am not sorry: I tried, I failed, the end.

I have shredded my copy of my Will, and although there may still be a copy in existence it is my wish at this time that my meager estate be divided equally between the parties copied below, with Joe and Bonnie Salvers to constitute one party together. Please be advised that if any one party attempts to claim sole executorship of said estate, that party will be entirely liable for the debt(s) I have accrued; in any case my creditors will most likely attempt to make someone answerable for that debt, something which I do regret. While it was my true intention to make good on all debts, both private and public, I simply lack the strength and resources to do so. Best bet in this scenario is to have any property removed from my residence at 711 E. Medio St., Apt. J, Long Beach, CA, before the rent runs out (which at the time of this writing is estimated to be August 31, 2013 on the month-to-month lease agreement with Ocean Realty), and divided by consensus, and my existence disavowed should anyone come asking.

I thank you for your kindnesses and consideration, at this time and in the past, and I wish you all the best.

Sincerely,

CC:
Margaret Crites
*(910) 738-****xxxx***
Thomas R. Crites
*(415) 719-****xxxx***
Joseph and Bonnie Salvers
*(626) 354-****xxxx***

P.S. Regarding the as-yet-unpublished PANISCUS REVUE book, for which the complete manuscript has been delivered, a contract has been signed, and an advance paid earlier this year, David Kerekes at Headpress in the UK is the point of contact for this; he can be reached at office@headpress.com.

After Words

Bonnie S.

Last Monday, one of my nearest and dearest friends passed away and this will be my only opportunity to eulogize him. I knew Tom Crites for twenty-three years and I can say that I never met a man who was as intellectual and low brow, as sarcastic, shitty and kind at the same time, a killer card player, great cook, massively well read, incredibly gifted at both writing and art, as he was. He was the true definition of a Renaissance Man. His only fault was that he could never see his own brilliance. He lived in Dorian Gray's two-way mirror world where we could all see him but all he could see was a distorted, twisted picture of himself. Tom's life and death are not teaching tools but I would hope, passionately, that the people in my life that I love and cherish would realize their own worth because I do not keep friends that are not incredibly special. Tom was definitely one of the most special to me.

Robin B.

I'm devastated to learn that Tom Crites passed away back on Monday the 19th of this month from an overdose of sleeping pills. Tom and I both published each other's work—he in my *Sleazy Slice* series (and the 13th cover of *Cinema Sewer*), and I in his *Malefact* zine. We never met in person, but we exchanged many emails and messages, and he always struck me as such a warm and gentle soul despite the stark coldness of his maddeningly perfect lines. Just an absolutely brilliant artist (and I don't heap such praise lightly), and one that dealt with challenging imagery that really appealed to me. Gonna miss you, Tom! Thank you so much for wandering into my life and making a positive impact. Your gorgeous work lives on in your stead.

Alkbazz G.

choqué et triste d'apprendre la disparition d'un chouette gars et un grand illustrateur et zineux outre atlantique, Tom Crites, we'll miss you man.

Herdoktor N.

Bad news, RIP Tom :(

Joe S.

On Monday the 19th of this month Tom passed away in his apartment in Long Beach. He was a funny sarcastic guy as well as a great friend that my wife and I knew for a little over 20 years and I miss him already. It will be very hard for us to get over this one because he was such a character as well as one hell of a talented artist. Someone like Tom comes around so seldom, we can only be thankful that we were able to share his company for a little while.

Johnny C.

SO sorry to hear such a phenomenal artist and nice guy is gone; his greater than great art lives on... *Malefact* remains one of my favorite zines ever... RIP Tom, you rock so damn hard!

Sergio Z.

Wow... just found out Tom Crites passed away. So sad. Never met the guy and didn't even knew he was such an amazing artist... I just knew him as a nice guy on FB that enjoyed my stupid art. I will miss his presence very much. RIP man.

Robert B.

This is the first time I ever lost a friend that I never met in person. A great writer and a good man. Tom Crites wrote for The Horror Review on and off for many years. He had great taste in film and books. He loved reviewing the worst of the worst and the best of the best. He kissed no one's ass in the business. If your film sucked he let you know in the most professional way possible. I used to get hate mail for him all the time, but I always took his side, because we tended to share the same opinion. He was once approached by a crazy filmmaker for giving their film a bad review; one he wrote for the site. I was so freaked out by it I took the review down. Tom did not blame me. He laughed about it at the end, but told me never to give his address to anyone. He got a PO Box after that. The last time we talked was not too long ago. He wished me luck on *Agoraphobia*. Tom was a great writer and a nice guy. I loved his reviews and nutty emails bitching about how horrible the films were that were sent to him for review. But he enjoyed every second of it and wrote full blown critiques like no other. So long my friend. Hopefully we will meet in spirit on the other side.

Antoinette R.

I am totally shocked and devastated by this news. Tom Crites was a friend and brilliant artist and he will be sorely missed. R.I.P. May your art live on!

Ken S.

My wife Anne (also a UCSB student and Tom's friend) and I moved to the Bay Area after college, lived near Tom and saw him all the time. As the years progressed and life took us to different locales, we always stayed in touch and we visited Tom many times in every town he lived in.

Although we didn't see each other in person very often in

recent years (Anne and I just returned to the U.S. from living in Cambodia for 6 years), we've always stayed in touch and I have always counted Tom among my very few, very closest friends and loved him like a brother. Tom's voracious appetite for learning and creativity have been an inspiration for me since the college days, an inspiration that is still very much a part of me today and which I continually try to emulate—admittedly without ever coming close to Tom's input and output!

Our hearts ache that Tom could not find a way to a happier existence, despite having good friends nearby like Joe and Bonnie and being very much loved from afar by Anne and me. He was very special to me and, although I have lost other friends, his death has hit me hardest. I will never forget him and I will miss him terribly for the rest of my life.

Vince B.

My fellow soldiers in the comic book community who will never apologize for our love of mature art have lost a gifted friend today.

Scott P.

i have known tom for almost 20 years. we first connected through the printed world, the independent magazine scene we were both part of so long ago. i came across his *malefact* magazine and soon after contacted him and we became friends almost instantly as we shared so much in common. i actually interviewed him for a magazine i was publishing when he was still out in virginia (is that right?) and soon after he moved out here to California. we've remained friends and on occasion we would still hang out and watch horror movies and cook some food.

to say that tom is an amazing and extremely talented artist is such an understatement. still to this day he remains one of the few artists i've come across where his abilities truly amaze me. his black and white pen work is simply out of this world. the lines, the attention to detail, the composition... all of it... incredible.

Wicked Art

To many people in this seedy existence known as the underground art world, Crites is a God. Established artists admire him as a leader in free expression and artistic style, and just mention his name to young underground artists and eyes grow wide. There are no words that one can condense together to describe the man the world has come to know and respect as Fuckin' Crites. You may find his incredible range of art work strange and perverse or sometimes dark and sinister, but he really was a very fuckin' cool guy.

Karen C.

I am so saddened every time I think about not having you in my life. I flash back to when we first met and all the shit in between then and now... I miss you so much you asshole.

Monte T.

I posted this, one of my occasional silly monster doodles for Tom, before I saw the unhappy news. Tom was an astonishing artist and he's an enormous loss. To his family and friends, my heart goes out to you, may you find solace and peace. Please archive his work and don't let it get scattered.

Stuart S.

RIP Crites. I didn't know Tom as Tom, just Crites. He didn't only produce awesome zines but his notes and letters that came with them were witty, funny, total keepers. The main thing I want to write is that Crites had friends all the way over here in Australia who will miss the hell out of him. Another one of the good guys went way too soon.

Stratu

Tom Crites did what?... Passed what now?... Crites (as I always knew him) has been one of my absolute favourite zine publishers from back in the late '90s when I was doing *Sick Puppy* and he had at that time both *Malefact* and *Paniscus Revue* on the boil. He was a great artist, but I really loved his writing, which could be found in his review zine, Paniscus Revue.

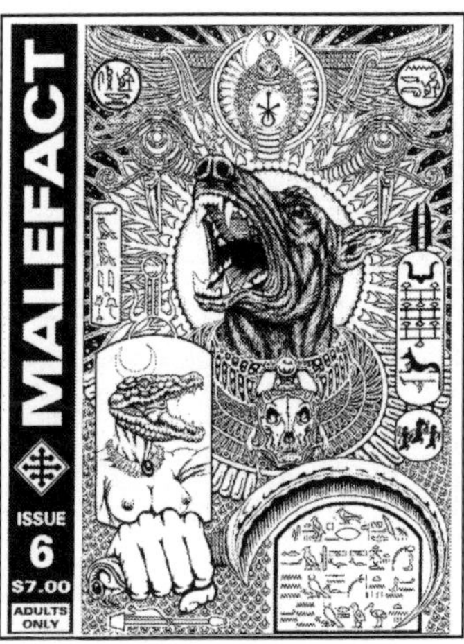

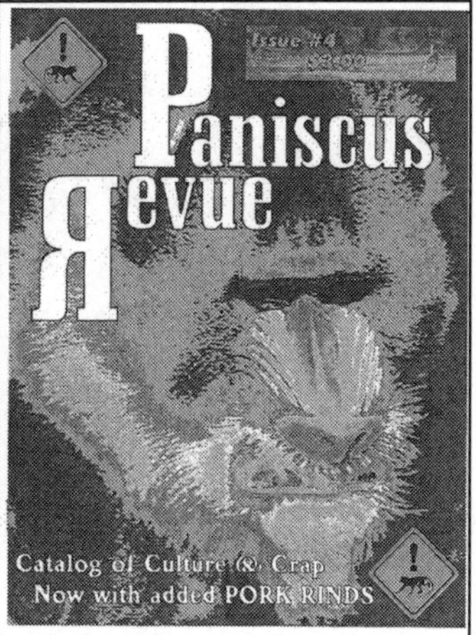

Marcel

So sad. *Malefact* and *Paniscus Revue* were among the very best things to appear from the fanzine scene in the 1990s.

Bruno

In memory of Tom Crites, who passed away on August 19. Tom was an amazing artist and tireless promoter of the sick and twisted in art and culture. I first started corresponding with Tom back in 1995, when he invited me to contribute to his magazine *Malefact*. This was in the pre-internet days of zines, when finding more extreme art and comics was still a difficult, word of mouth undertaking. *Malefact* was such a gorgeous mag; each issue was beautifully produced and crammed full of amazing art. It shone like a jewel on an inky heap of poorly-xeroxed scrawls, and I'm eternally grateful to Tom for reaching down into that heap and plucking my own work out of it. Tom's own artwork graced every cover, and it was always an eye-meltingly beautiful. The world needs more people like him. I'm really saddened by this news. RIP, Tom.

Gabe M.

This is a huge bummer. I still have old issues of *Malefact* that I insist on showing people when they ask what I wish more artists were doing. I always wanted someone to publish a collection of his work because his stuff was completely mind-blowing.

Elektrika P.
Goodbye Tom!

Acknowledgement

A special thanks to David Kerekes for his excellent editorial/publishing work on this manuscript. It would not have been possible to complete without his continued support and personal efforts.

Thank you David for bringing my son's work to light.